THE LORD IS...

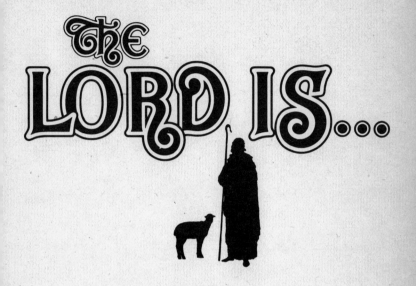

H. Edwin Young

BROADMAN PRESS
Nashville, Tennessee

WW10
Y85t

Scripture translations marked Moffatt are from *The Bible: a New Translation* by James A. R. Moffatt. Copyright © 1935 by Harper and Row, Publishers, Inc. Used by permission.

© Copyright 1981 ● Broadman Press
All rights reserved.
4215–26
ISBN: 0–8054–1526–2

Dewey Decimal Classification: 223.2
Subject heading: BIBLE. O.T. PSALMS
Library of Congress Catalog Card Number: 80–68750
Printed in the United States of America

To my wife
Jo Beth
and my sons
Ed, Ben, and Cliff

Introduction

Several pastorates ago, I planned a series of sermons based on the twenty-third Psalm for Sunday evenings. After a couple of weeks, I realized that these messages were Sunday-morning material. As I examined the phrases, and dissected each one carefully, I found an unexpected treasure—a serendipity. This familiar, favorite chapter was filled with a practical thrust for daily living, as well as doctrinal truths presented in a pastoral setting.

For over twenty-two years, I have prepared a manuscript for every Sunday morning sermon I have preached. So, the text for *The Lord Is . . .* was first written in the course of my weekly study. The response of the congregation gave me the idea that perhaps a book on the twenty-third Psalm could meet needs and reach people for the Shepherd. But the sermons were stored neatly in a file drawer and the project shelved.

Since the Psalm is a study in life situations, the

series seemed appropriate for "The Baptist Hour" audience when I was asked to deliver several weeks of messages as a guest speaker. I had preached from the twenty-third Psalm a short time before. The response during both of these times made me realize again how the passage speaks a fresh word . . . even to people who memorized the verses as children.

Through the years, this Psalm has become a part of my life. I have studied and examined its words and truths carefully. Although thoughts have come to light concerning the passage which were previously well hidden, covered from my realm of experience, or glossed over by familiarity, this message is clearly evident:

"The Lord is my shepherd" . . . but only when I let him lead.

And so, here is the result—a book which would not stay in the files! This work is presented with the prayer that the Lord will become your Shepherd too.

H. EDWIN YOUNG
Houston, Texas

Contents

Prologue

Charles Coburn, the late actor, once was asked how he managed to keep the lines in a play fresh and alive after weeks and sometimes months of reciting them almost daily. He explained that occasionally the play would be shut down for a time. The cast, the director, the musicians, all the production personnel, and even the writer would come together and read the play as though they had never heard it before.

Familiar Bible passages tend to lose their zest as we quickly scan them. "Oh, I know that. I've heard that all my life." However, when we apply Coburn's technique, the words become exciting again as they stir the depths of our being.

So let us approach the twenty-third Psalm, as though we had never heard it before.

The Lord is my shepherd; I shall not want. He maketh me to lie down in green pastures: he leadeth me beside the still waters. He restoreth my soul: he leadeth me in the paths of righteousness for his name's sake. Yea, though I walk through the valley of the shadow of death, I will fear no evil: for thou art with me; thy rod and thy staff they comfort me. Thou preparest a table before me in the presence of mine enemies: thou anointest my head with oil; my cup runneth over. Surely goodness and mercy shall follow me all the days of my life: and I will dwell in the house of the Lord for ever.

1

The
Lord Is . . .

"The Lord is my shepherd" (Ps. 23:1).

The words of the twenty-third Psalm are the possession of practically every educated mind in the English-speaking world. Since childhood, we have been familiar with this Psalm. Some of our earliest memories are linked with its beautiful phrases. As a boy I found the shepherd vocabulary strange. I did not understand what it all meant, but the beauty of the musical cadences and seventeenth-century English made an indelible impression. When I became a Christian, these words came alive. The difference? I then knew the Author, the Shepherd, Jesus Christ.

Dr. Charles Allen was counseling a nervous, tense man. This confused executive confessed that he had tried every prescription ordered by a score of physicians with no relief. After listening to the man's problem, Dr. Allen wrote another prescription: "Read the twenty-third Psalm five times a day for seven days."

The businessman was to read the Psalm carefully, meditatively, and prayerfully the first thing in the morning, immediately after breakfast, following lunch, after dinner, and, finally, before he went to bed. The amazing fact concerning this prescription was that it produced results.

Though the directions sound easy, they prove to be difficult. Absorbing the dynamics of these words will change a person's thought patterns. Proverbs 23:7 says, "For as he thinketh in his heart, so is he." Every time we go back to Psalm 23, we find new meaning. Familiarity only enhances God's truth in the Shepherd Psalm.

Every Christmas we hear Handel's *Messiah* without any sense of staleness. We know most of the music. Yet when we are receptive, some new meaning, undetected before, will find its entrance into our hearts and will be recognized for the first time.

This fact that is true of great art and literature is also true of David's Psalm. Listen as though you had never heard these words before: "The Lord is my shepherd." What does that mean? Inspired by God, David saw, through what he tried to do with his sheep in past days, a faint glimpse of how he was loved by God.

When trains were the usual way to travel long distances, a young family set out to visit relatives across the country. It was necessary for them to spend the night on board the train; therefore, Pullman accommodations were secured.

When bedtime arrived, the travelers discovered that their little five-year-old daughter could not sleep with her parents. Her berth was in the next compartment. Mom and Dad lovingly put Suzy to bed, assured her that they would be near, and told her to call if she needed anything. The strange surroundings and the idea that she could ask her parents to come soon prompted repeated cries, "Mother! Are you there? Daddy! Are you there?"

Trying to sleep in the berth next to the parents was a weary salesman, returning home from a convention. He could stand the disturbance no longer. "Yes," he retorted, "Mother's here! Daddy's here! Everybody's here! Let's all shut up and get some sleep!"

Suzy lay perfectly still. In a moment the night was broken with her question, "Daddy, was that God?"

Who is God? What is he like? His nature? His character? David, himself a shepherd, the son of a shepherd, and later known as "The Shepherd King," said, "The Lord is my shepherd." What did he mean?

He was talking about *Yahweh,* Jehovah, the Lord God of Israel. David's words of faith were later confirmed by Jesus Christ. In this Psalm God has the place of the shepherd; the writer, the place of the sheep. It is intriguing that the word *friend* in the Old Testament usually comes from the root of the word *shepherd.* Instantly, we observe what a tremendous compliment that first sentence is to the vocation of the shepherd. Remove the word *shepherd* and put in another word which also might be true in a figurative sense.

Perhaps a modern person would say, "The Lord is my grocer." But that simply does not seem to fit. A grocer has a good vocation. My dad was a grocer. There is nothing wrong with that profession! The Lord does provide for our daily needs, but the idea sounds flat.

Perhaps we could affirm, "The Lord is my physician." "Physician" has a ring to it. We recall the dignity which that profession has in our experience. Those vocations which we honor and respect most have about them an element of personal sacrifice in their service to mankind.

Jesus said, "I am the good shepherd: the good shepherd giveth his life for the sheep" (John 10:11). "The Lord is my shepherd." The biggest word in Psalm 23:1 is "Lord"; the next most important, "shepherd." Then there is the little word "my." Canon Bishop Green observed, "There is no emotion so necessary to a true religion nor any so fundamental to it, as a sense of being owned by God."

"The Lord is *my* shepherd." Look at this fourth word. Not only do we feel possessed by God but we also feel a sense of possessing him. Remember, David was a shepherd, but in this Psalm he thought of himself as a sheep—one of the flock. Pride and devotion are revealed. Literally, he was boasting, "Hey, look at who my shepherd is—my owner, my Lord."

A skilled shepherd can identify one of his sheep by

feeling its face. The sheep know the shepherd with equal intimacy. A shepherd might hang his cloak on his staff so that the sheep will not miss him. These animals can be deceived by sight, but not by sound. A stranger might trick the sheep by wearing a shepherd's clothing, but once the outsider tries to imitate the voice of the shepherd, the flock is immediately alerted.

Martin Luther stated that the heart of religion lies in its personal pronouns. Faith which is not personal is nothing. Jesus exemplified this fact as he spoke in intimate tenderness, "My sheep hear my voice, and I know them, and they follow me: And I give unto them eternal life; and they shall never perish, neither shall any man pluck them out of my hand" (John 10:27–28).

If I were told that a seven-year-old boy was reported lost in a wooded area, I would be concerned and interested in his welfare. However, if the message were that *my* seven-year-old son, Cliff, were lost, my concern and anguish would intensify! If this is true in a human relationship, how can we comprehend God's loving concern for us? I'll tell you how: "For God so loved the world that he gave his only begotten Son, that whosoever believeth in him should not perish, but have everlasting life" (John 3:16).

A few years ago, two Christian men were having a holiday in the Welsh mountains. As they sat to rest, far up in the hills, they began talking with a shepherd boy who was minding his sheep. They found he had missed the privileges of formal education. He had little knowledge of church or of Christianity. The travelers talked with him for awhile concerning who Jesus is and the simple truths of God. When they parted, the men instructed, "Just remember five words: 'The Lord is my shepherd.' Let each word," they reminded, "stand for the thumb and fingers on your left hand. Grasp them with your right hand, one by one, beginning with the thumb, as you say the words, 'The Lord is my shepherd.' "

The following year the two men were hiking in the same mountains and stopped at a cottage for a drink of fresh water. In the tiny Welsh home, they noticed a picture of a boy who seemed familiar. The lady of the house said, "Gentlemen, it seems unlikely that you would know the lad because it's a photograph of my son who was killed last winter. While going out after the sheep in a storm, he fell over a cliff. He lay there many hours on a ledge before he was found."

The two men then remembered that this definitely was the boy they had met the year before and quickly told the mother the circumstances. With a strange light in her eyes she exclaimed, "Why, Sir, perhaps you can explain something which has always puzzled me. When we found him, he was already dead. With his right hand, he was grasping tightly the third finger of his left hand."

"Yes," answered one of the men, "I can explain that." He told the mother what had happened when they had met her son on the mountain. The boy, gripping the third finger of his left hand, was simply emphasizing the fourth word of the phrase he had learned, "The Lord is *my* shepherd."

Think about it. With thousands of people, the third finger of the left hand bears a symbol which implies possession. A wedding ring, endless and precious, is placed on that finger in preference to others, supposedly because of an old legend. The legend taught that a nerve goes directly from this finger to the heart—the center, the seat of love. The gold ring I wear today was placed there when I could unreservedly say concerning the one I love, "She is mine."

Can you say, "The Lord is mine; the Lord is my shepherd"? Tragically, many people who have never really been under his direction or management make this claim. They hope that merely by proclaiming him to be their Shepherd, somehow they will enjoy the benefits of his management without paying the price of turning from their own sinful lifestyles. We cannot have it both ways: We belong or we do not belong.

Jesus warned that many will say, "Lord, . . . thy name [we did] many wonderful works" (Matt. 7:22). He will answer that he never knew us as his own.

Do you really belong to Christ? Do you find purpose because you are under his leadership? If you can answer yes, you may exclaim with confidence and pride, "The Lord is my shepherd!"

2

Everything
I Need

"The Lord is my shepherd; I shall not want. He maketh me to lie down in green pastures: he leadeth me beside the still waters" (Ps. 23:1–2).

About 150 years ago, an Englishman named Malthus identified the twin problems of population and production. He predicted that the world was moving toward global famine and mass starvation. The population was increasing at a faster rate than food was being produced. He could see the day coming when there would not be enough food. This scholar's prediction frightened many and precipitated a land-grabbing spree. Scientists debated Malthus and claimed that his facts were not accurate and that his total perspective and conclusions were based on the farming area of England.

People laughed and ridiculed the man who had underestimated the world's resources and man's resourcefulness. For many generations the world heard little about conservation. The Industrial Revo-

23

lution, mass production, the refrigeration of food, the opening of new continents, and many other events which Malthus did not perceive made the prophet's predictions seem ridiculous.

Today the ghost of Malthus walks. With food prices soaring and oil products secured only at a premium, the energy crisis is a practical consideration. Overpopulation and underproduction is beginning to haunt us as questions about the world's hunger often preoccupy our thoughts.

David exulted, "The Lord is my shepherd; I shall not want." *The Living Bible* paraphrases this verse: "Because the Lord is my Shepherd, I have everything I need!" Today the area in Palestine where David kept his sheep is one of the most barren places I have ever seen. Looking at it from a surface perspective, we readily agree that if sheep can eat rocks and stone, they will never be in want! Though the land was never lush, in David's day there were good grazing lands. These pastures were frequently far from the shepherd's home.

One of the toughest challenges a shepherd had was that of feeding his flock. David had been a shepherd himself. In spite of the fact that finding suitable pastures was often difficult, David looked to God and said: "I shall not want."

In our world today, where we are grappling with the twin problems of population and production, is this shepherd's word in the Scriptures some sentimental unreality? Is this the soaring stretching of a

poet's imagination? Or can we really take it seriously and believe that, because God is our Shepherd, we
shall not be in want?

What was Jesus talking about when he said, "Oh,
men, how little ye trust in him. Do not be troubled
then and cry, 'What are we to eat or what are we to
drink or how are we to be clothed?' Pagans make all
this their aim in life." Then Jesus said, "Your heavenly Father knows quite well you need all of that"
(Matt. 6:30–32, author's paraphrase).

I have visited the slums in cities around the world.
Remember Gandhi's statement? "Even God Himself
dares not appear to a hungry man except in the form
of bread." I have always found it impossible to tell
the hungry that they should trust God for their food.
When I see need, hunger, and privation, I always feel
challenged to be that medium through which God
fills those needs. However, we must never be guilty
of toning down God's response to his children's
prayers by the smallness of our faith in God's ability
to do for them all that needs to be done. In the face
of the world's waste and the world's want, we need
divine initiative, as well as human stewardship.

Under the guise of sophistication, I heard a man
laugh at the old story of Elijah being fed by the
ravens. If a collection were made of all the vivid
stories telling how men and women have received
direct help from God, it would form an impressive
display of indisputable evidence. People have prayed
to God and have received comfort and nourishment

which carried all the marks and signs of an immediate divine response to their petition.

Hugh Redwood relates story after story in his books of people reduced to a terrible poverty who have had definite material answers to their prayers. One of these is of a little slum boy who had no boots which were of the slightest use in wet weather. His mother, with no money to buy new ones, had been carrying him to and from school, rather than letting him walk through the wet streets. He seemed to be getting heavier each day. One evening she fell into a chair and cried because she was afraid she could carry him no longer. Alfie puckered up his little forehead and looked grave. "I'll have to tell Jesus about it," he said.

His mother, half-awed and half-amused, listened while he put the matter in plain, straightforward language before his Friend, "Dear Jesus, I have heard that you send other little boys shoes and things to wear. Please send some to me." Alfie had his supper and went to bed.

Although his parents had mentioned the need to no one, there was a knock at the door. It was their neighbor with a pair of boots which were getting too small for their young son but which would do splendidly for Alfie. The mother tiptoed back to Alfie's bedside and, because he was asleep, laid the boots beside him on the pillow. His shout awakened her in the morning. "Mother," he cried, "they have come and He knew my size too. And there is no hole in the ceiling."

We need to remember that our extremity is always the Lord's opportunity. I do not believe it is part of God's mind that one person should have more than enough for his needs and that another should be unable to clothe and feed his children. God wants his blessings to be shared. I wonder how many times there have been individuals who have cried out to the Father in want, but God has been hindered from supplying that want because of our selfish greed—our sin.

"The Lord is my shepherd; I shall not want." When David wrote these words, he was not referring merely to material poverty. This is primarily a spiritual assertion. As Christians we must recognize that our lives on this planet are brief interludes during which there may be deprivation in a physical sense. Yet in the middle of this hardship, we can still boast, "I shall not want. I shall not lack the expert care and management of my Master, the Good Shepherd."

Consider the phrase, "He maketh me to lie down." A shepherd writing from first-hand experience with sheep says that it is almost impossible to get them to lie down unless four basic requirements are met.

1. The sheep are free from fear.
2. They are free from friction with others.
3. They are free from flies and parasites.
4. They are free from hunger.

How like sheep we are! If we are to be at rest, there

must be within our lives a definite sense of freedom from fear, friction, aggravations, and hunger. The unique aspect of the picture is: it is only the shepherd who can provide release from these problems and anxieties. The flock's freedom from disturbing influences depends on the diligence of their owner.

"The Lord is my shepherd; I shall not want. He maketh me to lie down." Where? "In green pastures." Green pastures do not merely happen! They are the product of tremendous labors of clearing rough, rocky land, of tearing out brush, roots, and stumps, of plowing and soil preparation, of seeding and planting special grains. Irrigation is necessary. These efforts represent acts of love by a good shepherd.

An ill-fed sheep is always on its feet and on the move, searching for another mouthful of foliage, trying to satisfy its gnawing hunger. Hungry sheep are not contented and do not thrive. Lacking vigor and vitality, they are of no use to themselves or to their owners.

Many of us resemble restless sheep. We have difficulty being still or sleeping because we cannot find peace. We are hungry for something and are always on the move. A clear picture of the present condition of this generation includes push and pull, hustle and pressure.

Alvin Toffler in his book *Future Shock* wrote that everything is changing. I do not believe it is possible to live in our modern society unless there is a change

which only the Good Shepherd, Jesus Christ, can
bring about. That change is within the heart of human beings.

Augustine said, "Thou has made us for thyself,
and our hearts are restless until they find rest in
Thee." If you do not have a living relationship with
Christ, you can never find green pastures or still
waters and you can never lie down with the confidence that the Shepherd of life is in control of your
destiny. This life of quiet overcoming, of rest in his
presence, of confidence in his management, is the life
far too few Christians ever enjoy. Many of us prefer
to forage on the barren ground of the world around
us.

"He leadeth me beside the still waters." Sheep
cannot swim. If they could, the task would be comparable to a person swimming with his overcoat on!
So a sheep is frightened by rushing waters. In Palestine there are not many clear springs which are still.
During the rainy season, the water flows swiftly. At
other times, most of the streams are dry altogether.

When the water was abundant, the shepherd
would find a little spring. He would then dig a cis-
tern, prepare it with rock, and cover the water which
would fill the underground container. Then in the
hot summer season, he would lead his sheep to the
cool, clear water as a relief from the scorching sun.

In another passage, the psalmist said, "As the hart
panteth after the water brooks" (Ps. 42:1). A hot,
panting deer standing over a stream does not make

sense! To translate the phrase "as the hart panteth over the aqueduct" seems more accurate. Aqueducts were large, underground caverns. The picture is of a deer standing over an aqueduct. A little hole allows him to smell the water. He stands there exhausted, panting and moaning for the water which he cannot reach.

Instead of letting the Good Shepherd remove the cover so we may drink freely of his cool, refreshing water, our lives have become agitated and frantic. We can identify with the story of a lady who had two cats. One day her husband was showing their house to a stranger. As they went through the kitchen, the man noticed two flaps in the wall. Obviously, some animal used these holes as exits. He questioned the owner.

"You see, my wife has two cats. They go in and out through these holes."

"But I don't understand. Wouldn't one hole have been enough?"

The head of the household replied, "Listen, fellow, when my wife says, 'Scat,' she means, 'Scat!' "

I wonder if the picture of lying down in green pastures, of being led by still waters, speaks to us today? Is it not a reminder for us to "be still and know that I am God" (Ps. 46:10)? Once Jesus asked a question which none of us should forget for a single day, "For what is a man profited, if he shall gain the whole world, and lose his own soul?" (Matt. 16:26).

A minister walked into the busy office of a friend,

the owner of a large company. Everybody was in a
mad rush! As the pastor walked in, three men ran
out before he could speak a word. A clerk rushed in
and shoved a paper to be signed in front of the executive, jerked it away, and hurried out. The intercom
buzzed. The man of authority said, "Just a minute."
He picked up the receiver and gave orders to some-
body else. Everyone seemed to be moving in and out
in quick double-time. All the typewriters clattered.
The sound of computers echoed in the distance.
Doors banged. The place was in total disorder.

The pastor related that he sat quietly for two or
three minutes before his friend looked up and asked,
"What's on your mind, Preacher?" Then the executive continued writing.

The minister recalled, "I just sat there and began
to quote in a low voice: 'Let not your heart be troubled, neither let it be afraid.' 'In my Father's house
are many mansions: if it were not so, I would have
told you.' 'Come unto me, all ye that labour and are
heavy laden, and I will give you rest.' 'The Lord is my
shepherd; I shall not want. He maketh me to lie
down in green pastures: he leadeth me beside the
still waters.' "

As the minister quoted a little further, his friend's
face relaxed. He leaned back in his chair with a
facial expression resembling a little boy nestled in
his mother's arms. When the visitor arose and
started toward the door, the contemplative executive
said, "Pastor, come back again and do it all over."

There is a time for rest, and there is a time for activity. The same Jesus who said, "Come ye yourselves apart . . . and rest a while" (Mark 6:31) also said, "Go unto all the world" (Mark 16:15). If Jesus is our Shepherd, then we need to listen to him, to trust him, and to meet him regularly.

A young mother had five children. Times were hard, and there was never enough money. When all the pressures of life closed in around her, she disappeared for a few moments. From a very early age her children noticed that when she returned, there was a new joy and glow about her.

In time the oldest daughter married and had a family of her own. She wrote home to her mother: "Dear Mom, All those years I wondered where you went when we were arguing and fussing. Now that I have children, I have discovered that you went away to be with God in prayer."

I do not believe it possible to live the Christian life unless we have regular sacred times for the green pastures and the still waters. This communion comes only when the Lord Jesus Christ is our Shepherd.

3

The
Power of
Restoration

"He restoreth my soul" (Ps. 23:3).

These four, simple words express a lovely pastoral picture. Actually, we could reduce these four words to three. The word translated "soul" is merely a synonym for *me*. There is no dualism in the Scriptures between soul and body. If a man lives, the whole of that person lives. If a man dies, the whole of that person dies. The dualism that has seeped into the church comes not from the Scriptures, but from Plato. There is absolutely no difference between the word *soul* in this Scripture and the word *body*.

Moffatt translates this verse: "He revives life in me." We must remember that here a sheep in the Good Shepherd's care is speaking. But why this word? It is hard to imagine that a sheep cared for by a good shepherd would fall into trouble. Yet this fact remains—It has happened to us.

David, who was loved by God, knew what it meant to be cast down and rejected. He had tasted defeat and had felt the frustration and estrangement of sin. The shepherd king was acquainted with bitterness and with feeling helpless and powerless, without strength in himself.

In Psalm 42:11, David cried out: "Why art thou cast down, O my soul? and why art thou disquieted within me?"

"He restoreth my soul" could be read, "He found me when I was cast down and gave life to me again." If we are familiar with sheep and their habits, we understand the significance of a "cast sheep" or a "cast-down sheep." The term, *cast-down sheep* is an old English shepherd's term for a sheep who has turned over on its back and cannot get up again by itself.

This is what happens. A heavy, fat, or long-fleeced sheep will lie down comfortably in a little hollow or depression in the ground. It rolls on its side slightly to stretch and relax. Then the center of gravity in the body shifts. The sheep turns on its back so the feet no longer touch the earth. As it rolls over even further, it can become impossible for the sheep to turn upright. The sheep is "cast down." Usually the largest and strongest sheep are the most easily cast. If the weather is extremely hot and sunny, a cast-down sheep may be in critical condition within a few hours. If it is cool, cloudy, or rainy, it may survive in this position for several days.

The owner must arrive on the scene within a reasonably short time or the sheep could die. For this reason, a shepherd must watch his flock carefully, counting the sheep to see that all are up and on their feet. If one or two sheep are missing, the first thought in a shepherd's mind is, *One of my sheep is cast down somewhere. I must go and search and set it on its feet again.*

All of God's concern is contained in the simple phrase, "He restoreth my soul." Many have the idea that when a Christian sins, God gets mad. This is not true. One of the great revelations given to us by Jesus is that God is our Shepherd. The Lord has the same sensations of anxiety, concern, and compassion for cast men and women that a shepherd has for cast sheep.

Once a despondent man contemplated suicide. He considered every method he knew: "I could shoot myself, take poison, hang myself, burn myself, or drown myself." To be absolutely sure that the task would be accomplished, he decided to use all the procedures at the same time. His rationale was, "If I'm going to kill myself, I'll do it in such a way that the coroner will never figure out what did the job."

He climbed into a small boat and pushed it out onto a lake. Next, he put his head through a hangman's noose in a rope which he had placed over a limb. He cocked a loaded pistol and put it to his head. He doused himself with gasoline and, just as he put a match to his body, he drank the poison.

Suddenly, he slipped on the boat seat and accidentally pulled the trigger—the bullet severed the rope.

This caused him to fall into the water, which put out the fire. As he went down, he swallowed so much of the stagnant lake water that he became sick and regurgitated the poison. Later he commented, "If I hadn't been such a good swimmer, I would've drowned!"

Tragically, many give up on life and destroy themselves. A more widespread disaster is evident in those who have lost all purpose for living. Many continue to breathe and function but are not really alive.

Jesus cares. This fact is noted time and again during his earthly ministry as he demonstrated compassion and love. It explains his dealing in relationships of love with down-and-out individuals for whom even human society had no use. This tells us why he cried over those who laughed at his suffering. It discloses the depths of his understanding of discouraged people to whom he came eagerly and quickly to save, to forgive, and to restore. Read the life of Jesus afresh, and notice the many times he tenderly dealt with fallen humans—like a good shepherd picking up cast-down sheep.

Peter boasted, "Everybody else might run, but 'the rock' will be here! You can count on me; I'll give my life for you."

Jesus replied, "Peter, before the cock crows you will deny me three times."

When the men came to take Jesus from the garden, Peter drew his sword and cut an ear off of a servant of the high priest (John 18:10). Impetuous Peter was saying with this act, "Look at me! I'm standing up to these men! They're not going to take my Master!" But they led Jesus away.

Later, Peter was by the fire, outside of the place of Jesus' trial. A young girl spoke, "This man was with the prisoner."

"I don't know him," he replied.

"You're one of them."

"No, I am not."

"You surely were with him. You are from Galilee. I can tell by your accent!"

This time Peter cursed as he denied ever knowing Jesus.

The rooster crowed, and Peter remembered. Then he "went out and wept bitterly."

After the resurrection, some of the disciples were fishing. In fact, they had been at work all night with no results. Jesus instructed them to throw their nets on the other side of the boat. The resulting catch was tremendous. At that moment, Peter recognized the Lord and swam to the shore to see him.

When Peter arrived, Jesus had a fire ready to prepare breakfast. "Bring some fish you've caught, and we'll cook them."

After they had eaten, Jesus looked at Peter and asked him a simple question, "Simon, do you love me more than you love all these other things?"

"Yeah, yeah, I love you."

Then Jesus answered, "Feed my sheep. Simon, do you really love me as a friend?"

"Yes, Lord, you're a close friend. You know I love you."

"Feed my lambs. Simon, do you really love me?"

"Yes, Master."

"Then feed my little sheep."

Three times he denied; three times he confessed (John 21:15–17). The Good Shepherd came ministering and brought Peter back into the fold. Jesus restored him as a shepherd would bring a once-cast sheep back into the flock.

This verse can be translated, "He restoreth my soul" or "He revives life in me," but perhaps the best translation is, "He brings me back from wandering." An old law in Palestine stated that if an animal strayed from the care of its owner onto the land of another and remained there for a period of twenty-four hours, it could never be reclaimed by its original owner. The animal would become the property of the person onto whose land it had wandered.

The finder of a lost sheep would often cut its throat and claim the carcass if it were cold before the shepherd reached it. A shepherd would frequently break the leg of a sheep which habitually strayed to prevent it from being lost. The compassionate shepherd would then pick up the crippled sheep and carry it around on his back day after day until the leg was restored and strong again.

With this law in mind and remembering the hostility and rivalry which existed between landowners in Palestine, we should not be surprised to discover that these men would try any sort of trick imaginable to acquire possession of sheep. Sometimes a deep pit would be dug and covered over to look exactly like the surrounding area. A wandering animal would fall into the hole and become a prisoner. If the owner readily found his sheep (or other animal), all was well. However, if witnesses proved that the animal had been in the pit longer than one day, it could not be reclaimed.

This situation puts new light on the words of Jesus in Matthew 12:11: "What man shall there be among you, that shall have one sheep, and if it fall into a pit on the sabbath day, will he not lay hold on it, and lift it out?" If a man had waited until after the sabbath, it would have been too late; the sheep would have become the property of the other landowner. The law of property was so scrupulously observed in those days that the rigid sabbath rules made provision for lost animals. Sheep owners could search for these and do whatever was necessary for full recovery.

In Luke 15 is the parable of the shepherd who searched for the one lost sheep until it was found and then returned with the animal on his shoulders. We can imagine the shepherd calling for his missing possession as he scoured the area. After being found, the sheep needed no coaxing to go with his master.

Jesus said, "My sheep hear my voice, and I know

them, and they follow me" (John 10:27). The only people who have ever experienced failure with Jesus Christ are those who never trust him. I have never heard a single person say, "I've tried Christianity, but it does not work." Do you know anybody who says, "My life is in shambles because I have been a follower of Jesus Christ"? Have you ever heard anybody say, "I'm all filled with guilt, and I can't sleep at night because I read my Bible and study it every day"? Or, "I regularly worship the Lord and spend time in meditation and adoration of him, and I'm all confused"?

I am baffled by people who turn their backs on Jesus Christ and continue to wander around on dead-end streets, rejecting everything. They have never really tried being Christian and living the Christian life for a period of time. The amazing fact about God's path is that it leads to life. Many roads running around this world look very alluring, but every one either runs out to a ledge or ends in a bog of wilderness. Only God can return us to him.

Some basic principles can help us guard against being "cast down." Recall the fact that a sheep will search for a soft place where it can lie comfortably. The Christian is always in danger when he looks for the easy life where there is no need for endurance or demand for self-discipline.

Then remember that a sheep with a very long, heavily matted fleece is easily cast. "Wool" in the Scriptures denotes the old self-life in the Christian, an outward expression of an inner attitude. A Christian gets in trouble when he clings to an accumulation of worldly notions and ideas. These "things" hold him down. An interesting fact is that the high priest could never wear wool when he entered the holy of holies. Such a garment spoke of self and pride —attitudes which God would not tolerate.

The third chief cause of cast sheep is their size: a fat sheep is easily cast. Fat sheep are neither the healthiest nor the most productive. These are put on a diet! The Christian who has achieved and has a great degree of well-being and self-assurance is in danger. Jesus spoke of a wealthy farmer who planned to build bigger barns and rest at ease. His days were numbered. "This night thy soul shall be required of thee."

"He restoreth my soul." It is important that we put the emphasis on God in the words, "He restoreth." We need God as sheep need a shepherd. Being a Christian is not simply instinctive, though some of its roots are instinctive. The sheep, unlike some other animals, have no inborn urge to go home. No "natural man" has an overwhelming desire to be one with God. In fact, the exact opposite is true. We want to be autonomous and independent. We set out without track, plan, or chart. We follow the wrong path. Now for the first few miles, we experience the exuberant hilarity of those who have broken with all laws and restraint. The sad fact is that often we are making good time, but we never arrive anywhere.

We become lost and need to come back. Some become lost and never return.

Hunger is an instinctive urge, driving us to eat; but there is nothing completely comparable to physical appetite in our spiritual lives. I think that this is a sign of God's respect for our personalities. He does not want us to seek him merely because we are forced or driven by some inner compulsion. Such a design would make us puppets.

Our power to run away from God and our power to follow God both come from him. If we seek him, we do not have far to go. For it is not the sheep who find the Shepherd: the Shepherd finds the sheep. His journey began before ours. "Behold, I stand at the door, and knock" (Rev. 3:20). We are disturbed because he is near. We come to him because he calls. If we love him at last, it is because he first loved us and came close enough to make it known. Now, if we cannot find the Good Shepherd, the hindrance is ours. He alone can bring us back from wandering. "And I will restore to you the years that the locust hath eaten" (Joel 2:25).

4

The
Right Path

"He leadeth me in the paths of righteousness for his name's sake" (Ps. 23:3).

The inscription on a plaque at Florida's Singing Towers states, "I come here to find myself. It is so easy to get lost in the world."

How true! Literally or figuratively speaking, getting on the wrong road is a frustrating, time-consuming experience. Staying on the right road of life can be accomplished only through following the Lord's directions.

"He leadeth me in the paths of righteousness for his name's sake." This verse could be rendered, "He leads me in the true paths for the sake of his name." *The International Critical Commentary* presents it: "In right tracks." Moffatt translates it, "He guides me by true paths, as he himself is true." We would express it, "He keeps me on the right track." David remembered his own experiences as a shepherd. He knew that sheep have no sense of direction. Many

other animals do, but sheep do not. The picture behind these words is one with which every shepherd
is familiar.

The shepherd psalmist was saying that God guided
by walking ahead of him on the right path. Left on
their own, sheep tend to wander around and become
lost easily. In the Mideast, a shepherd walks in front
of the sheep. He makes sure that the paths are wide
enough for all the sheep to follow comfortably. In the
Western world, the shepherd walks behind his sheep
because the paths or trails are more easily defined
and because the terrain is not as rugged or as
marked with cliffs and precipices.

"He leads me in the right path to uphold his
name" is a possible rendering. We of the Christian
faith categorically state that we believe in divine
guidance. The secular world says, "You mean to tell
me that God in heaven speaks to you? Have you ever
heard God speak audibly?"

This generation has difficulty understanding such
truth for two basic reasons: magnitude and communication. Mark Twain wrote that he did not believe God knows we are here! The universe is too
large for any person to fully comprehend.

According to a story, two men had the awesome
adventure of being lost in space and landing on a
distant planet. They found the natives friendly
enough but lacking in understanding. "Where do
you come from?" the natives questioned.

"Why, we are from Earth," the men replied.

"Earth? What is that?"

"You know, the planet Earth," they answered, and proceeded to explain as best they could.

"Oh, yes. We know of that place. We call it 'the wart.' "

Since light travels at 186 thousand miles per second, it requires 50 million years for the light from a distant star to come into our view. We are seeing light from a few stars which have already burned out! In a cosmos so vast, how could God be interested in whether I take that job or whether I have personal problems or relationships?

Perhaps the difficulty in understanding divine guidance lies in communication. How can a people who do not adequately communicate with each other receive direction from God? As Christians, we declare firmly that God does guide us by faith. This truth is found in the total witness of the Bible.

How then do we receive God's direction? How does he keep us on the right track? Our road map of the "right path" is the Bible. This Book is salvation history—it is the Word of God. Through its pages we find the mind of God.

A fellow once explained how he found what God wanted him to do. He remarked to me, rather impressively, "I just take my Bible, open it at random, and where my finger falls, God speaks."

I told him of another person who used the same method. He said, "Lord, speak to me," and put his finger on the verse, "and [Judas] went and hanged

himself" (Matt. 27:5) This statement did not seem
appropriate, and so he turned over several pages and
read, "Go and do thou likewise" (Luke 10:37).

Although this helter-skelter method is not ade-
quate for guidance, nevertheless the Word of God is
a lamp unto the feet of the believer. Passages must
be considered in context and in the light of the total
biblical record. Through a more thorough approach
to study, we find God's direction.

Furthermore, there are times when God uses the
fellowship of the church to reveal his will. I have
seen numerous individuals discover answers
through prayer within some group in the church.
The message of God is in the hearts of his gathered
community. A person shares his concerns with
Christian friends, and they combine their knowledge
and prayer power. Thus, God makes his plans and
purposes known.

We also receive direction by using our common
sense. One person remarked, "I prayed about a problem and never did get an answer. And so I used my
common sense, and everything came out perfectly."
God is a part of our common sense too! He works in
our reasoning processes: our common sense. He is
inside of us already. We must let his Spirit break out!

Another way God speaks to us is through what the
Quakers call "Inner Light." The truth comes to us
from within. Samuel answered, "Speak, [Lord] for
thy servant heareth" (1 Sam. 4:10). We say, "Listen,

Lord, for thy servant speaketh." We must learn to listen.

A grade-school teacher was having difficulty with her students. There were so many discipline problems that she could not challenge the children to reach their potential. One day she had an idea. As the class began, she said, "I want all of you boys and girls to bow your heads and see if God will say anything to you."

Thus she started class day after day. Over a period of six months, the change in the students was dramatic. The children reported what God said to them. "God told me not to cheat on my math test anymore." "God said I should mind my mother and daddy." "God told me to listen better in school."

The 'Inner Light' is present; we must take time to listen. "They that wait upon the Lord shall renew their strength; they shall mount up with wings as eagles; they shall run, and not be weary; and they shall walk, and not faint" (Isa. 40:31).

Sometimes we receive the wrong answer when we rely exclusively on our Inner Light. A particular "revelation" or "voice from God" should be examined in conjunction with other ways of the Lord's guidance. Any "light" which is contrary to Bible teaching is false. God will not tell a person to do something which is in disobedience to his written Word. The various avenues for discerning God's will, his direction, are used as a type of check-and-balance system. His leadership becomes clear to the true seeker.

Browning was right: "Every bush is alive with God." He is speaking, and we do not even know it! On occasion, the Lord breaks through in a special demonstration. There have been divine times in my life when the only explanation for an experience was, "God spoke to me."

A little boy once asked his mother if he could go out and play "catch" with God. "Now how in the world do you think you can play 'catch' with God?" she asked in amazement.

"Why, that's easy," the boy replied. "I throw the ball up, and he throws it back!"

We are reminded of Jesus' desire that we come to him as little children. His plan for our lives becomes clearer as we know him more intimately.

A young girl in an orphanage was cared for by a man whom she did not know and had never seen. Her every need had been met by this wonderful person. He showered her with gifts: delicious delicacies from distant places, diaphanous frocks covered with exquisite lace and ribbons, baubles of all sorts, as well as her day-by-day necessities.

Through the years, this generous man exhibited his love and care without being recognized or known by the girl. Only once she saw his shadow, and from that moment she affectionately called him "Daddy Longlegs" because his shadow made him appear tall and lean. She finally met her "Daddy Longlegs" and fell in love with him.

In Exodus 33, the account is given of another person who saw only the back of the One who gave him provision and direction. After the children of Israel had made the golden calf and had been disciplined because of that terrible deed, God told Moses that it was time to move on. The place of worship was outside the camp, and those "which sought the Lord" (Ex. 33:7) went to worship. Moses went out to talk with God. There he received the assurance that God was going with them.

However, Moses wanted more: he wanted to see God's face. Since it is not possible for anyone to see God's face and live, God put Moses in a hole within the rock and covered the opening with His hand. After his glory passed by, God permitted Moses to see his back. From this experience of a renewed vision, this liberator moved forward with the people.

Rarely do we see God as he moves into our lives. Many times we do not know that he is present in a precise moment. We, like Moses, see only the back of God. We know that he was present in the events of our lives only as we look back at our past experiences.

All our years we have been sustained by One who cares for us. He does not advertise or demand recognition. He simply gives to us from his treasures. Those who know him, love him. If we could only discover his desire to guide our lives . . . !

Does it seem strange that God is in the business of giving direction to those things which he has made? Every creation has a built-in guidance system. The giant oak tree has the ability to reproduce itself. A small acorn falls to the ground. Roots begin to go down into the soil, fighting for moisture and nourishment. A tiny green shoot appears and reaches upward to the heavens for light and air. A certain species of swallow spends the summer in England where it builds its nest and raises its young. When winter comes, it flies to South Africa, then, back to England and the same nest! The golden plover winters in Argentina and flies to the Arctic for the summer, a trip of some 8,000 miles. It makes a nonstop flight of around 2,500 miles of this journey over water. Scientists have tried to discover why it is impossible to lose a homing pigeon. This bird always returns amazingly and unerringly to its home. We can also be guided by the Lord. "In all thy ways acknowledge him, and he shall direct thy paths" (Prov. 3:6).

A family planned a picnic. The children insisted that all their friends and several neighbors be invited. The mother frantically got together their favorite treats and fried a large platter of chicken. Then they went out, found a cool, shady spot, and opened the lunch. After devouring lunch, the adults sat around and talked while the children went off to play. One dad warned, "Hey, don't go past that fence! Play in this area. Don't cross the fence!"

But what did the children do? They approached the fence with utmost caution, at first. Then, when no one was looking, over the fence they went! The older folk were deeply engaged in conversation by then and didn't seem to notice.

Things were even better on that side of the fence. What did Mom and Dad know anyhow? And so, the children ran and played—and found another fence which they promptly vaulted. Several fences and hedges later, darkness surrounded the children, and they had that sick, lost feeling. They called for their parents but heard no answers. Then they argued with one another about the right way to get back to the family.

The world of today reminds me of that scene. Individuals, groups, and countries wander off. They cross fences, traditions, and principles as they rebel and disregard their ancestors' warnings, "Go in this way." They say, "I'm not going to believe that. I'll go my own way." The road gets dark and then the realization comes: "This path does not lead anywhere, except over a steep precipice or into a boggy swamp." And they fight and argue concerning their next move.

Men of faith in Old Testament days—Noah, Abraham, Isaac, Jacob, Moses, and scores of others—were led by God on the right path. Jesus received direction from his Father. Those who have found themselves in the wilderness of modern times know of the Lord's guidance. He leads us for his name's sake: His reputation is at stake. He will always direct us in the right path.

When the compass was first introduced, it changed the limits of navigation. Until that time sailors kept their vessels close to the shore, using the stars for direction or watching landmarks along the coastline. This device enabled ships to go through uncharted courses without any indicator outside the vessel.

Jesus Christ gives inner guidance to those who let him enter their lives and have control. Yet, we are often like the executive who became lost every time he went hunting. His staff gave him a compass since they feared for his safety on his excursions. The following Saturday he went out again—and got lost, as usual! His employees questioned him, "What happened? Didn't you take your compass?"

"Oh yes," he answered, "but that thing didn't work. I started walking north, and the compass pointed southeast. It doesn't work!"

We have the source of direction at hand but choose to follow our own plan. Have you ever heard anybody say, "I've been reading my Bible and praying every day, and my life is all fouled up"? or, "I've been following Jesus Christ to the best of my ability, trying to live in freedom and joy, in fellowship with him, and I've made so many bad decisions"? His way works! Those who refute it have not experienced it for themselves.

In his book, *I Will Lift Up Mine Eyes,* Glenn Clark writes that for many years he had wanted to write an inspirational book. Each time he tried, the pen would freeze in his hand. Then he heard another author, Marian McGraw, share her story. She had also wanted to write, but somehow she could not. In her dilemma, she discovered a little verse in the Psalms: "He maketh my feet like hinds' feet, and setteth me upon my high places" (Ps. 18:33). She remarked that after she received her hinds' feet, the inspiration flowed.

Following the lecture, Clark rushed backstage to question this writer. What did she mean? What do hinds' feet have to do with writing? But she was gone.

Later, Clark was on the verge of nervous collapse. For therapy he went to a ranch and worked as a cowhand. One morning the foreman said, "Get your pony, and ride with us. We're going up in the hills, to Mesa #6, to take some salt to the cattle."

And so he rode with the cowboys up to Mesa #1, then #2, and all the way to Mesa #5. At this point the foreman said, "Dr. Clark, you'll have to stay here. You can't reach the top of Mesa #6."

"Why? Why can't I go along?"

"You see, the path is rocky and dangerous. And your horse doesn't track. Look. Watch my horse." Then he demonstrated. "The front feet lift up, and the hind feet fall exactly where the front feet were. My horse is surefooted; he runs like a deer."

Then Clark remembered, "He maketh my feet like hinds' feet."

"That's OK." he replied, "you go on. I have something to think about."

He got down on his knees and prayed, "Lord, I should take off my shoes because this is holy ground. Forgive me for not following you. My life just doesn't track. My rhythm and coordination are gone. Make my feet like hinds' feet."

Clark went home. The tug-of-war which had been in his life was not there anymore. He had the freedom to write.

At the end of a person's life, we might hear any number of statements about the deceased: "Mr. Smith left $50,000." "Dr. Jones could pull teeth better than anyone in town." "Mr. Charles was the shrewdest lawyer in the state." "Miss Nelson was the most competent teacher I knew." "Mr. Abbott played golf better than anyone else in the club."

I remember hearing a lady remark, "Isn't Mr. Bond wonderful? He knew every card in my hand last night at bridge."

Then someone else replied, "Has it ever occurred to you that Mr. Bond is forty-five and bridge is all that he knows?"

Make sure the path you choose leads you at last to a place where you want to be. A careful traveler will study the road map before setting out!

"In all thy ways acknowledge him, and he shall direct thy paths" (Prov. 3:6).

5

Terrified
By Tunnels

"Yea, though I walk through the valley of the shadow of death, I will fear no evil: for thou art with me" (Ps. 23:4).

A little girl was terrified by tunnels. She frequently traveled on a train with her family. Every time they approached a tunnel, she would press her face against her mother the moment the train entered the tunnel and would look up only when assured they were once again out in the sunshine.

A few years later, her fear had completely disappeared. While driving along the Pennsylvania Turnpike, the child was thrilled as they passed through the tunnels. Her mother, remembering the child's former fear, asked what made the difference. The little girl replied, "Mother, I like tunnels because they have a light at both ends."

This is the fact God wants us to discover about all valleys, as well as all tunnels: If God is with us, there is light at both ends.

"Yea, though I walk through the valley of the shadow of death, I will fear no evil: for thou art with me" (Ps. 23:4). From a shepherd's perspective, this statement marks the halfway stage in the twenty-third Psalm. Up to this point the sheep has been on the home range, boasting to his neighbor about the excellent care he receives from his owner. In this verse the sheep turns, not to its neighbor, but to the shepherd directly. Notice that the personal pronoun "thou" enters the conversation.

Winter and spring have ended. As summer begins, the shepherd leads the sheep to the high hill country. There the grass is green and the nourishment is plentiful. During this period the flock is in intimate contact with the shepherd and under his personal supervision day and night.

David the psalmist knew this type of experience firsthand. Remember when Samuel was sent by God to anoint David as king of Israel? He was not at home with his brothers. He was high in the mountains looking after his father's flock.

The shepherd boy never took his flock anywhere he had not already been himself. All the dangers of flooding rivers, rockslides, poisonous plants, blinding storms of sleet, hail, and snow were familiar to David. He had handled his sheep and managed them with care under every weather condition. Nothing took him by surprise. Likewise in every dark trial, in every dismal disappointment, in every distressing dilemma, the Christian can say, "I will [not] fear

. . . : for thou art with me."

A fire destroyed Thomas Edison's laboratory. Many unfinished experiments were burned beyond recognition. The scientist, while walking through the wreckage, found a little package of papers tied together tightly with a string. The package was water-soaked and fire-scarred, but by some freak of chance it was left secure. Thomas Edison opened it. At the center of the wrappings was a photograph of himself which was burned around the edges, but still undamaged. He looked at it for a little while. Then he picked up a piece of charcoal from the floor and wrote across the face of the picture: "It didn't touch me."

The psalmist said, "I will fear no evil: [because the Lord is my shepherd]." David was being autobiographical in this verse. He had an inner assurance that the scarring, burning, searing evils of life could never touch him. Let this truth soak in for awhile: Because God is our shepherd, nothing, not even the shadow of death, can touch us!

As a young boy, David had stood in the shadow of death. His faith was verified as he approached Goliath. David was perhaps the most unlikely person to be used by God. We can imagine what David was like.

Perhaps both of his parents had been previously married. David may have played with his father's grandchildren.

David may have had an IQ of 160-plus. He had the

poetic genius of a Shakespeare, the musical ear of a
Beethoven, the hand and eye coordination of a Bjorn
Borg, coupled with a military genius which has never been duplicated in history. David's childhood may
have been like that of a tremendously gifted boy
being reared with brothers who never finished the
third grade, had no poetic intuition, whose only
musical instrument was the bass drum, who had
never learned to walk and chew gum at the same
time, and whose military acumen vanished when the
club was superceded.

A student of personality development might conclude that David's home environment had the poten-
tiality of producing a super criminal. The secret of
his fearlessness was found in his preparation for bat-
tle with Goliath. Approaching Goliath, David picked
up five, smooth stones. Why did he pick up five
stones? Someone suggested it was the custom of the
day—like three strikes in baseball, two serves in ten-
nis, or four downs in football. Another person mentioned that the extra stones were probably for
Goliath's four brothers! I do not think that David
ever did anything as important as this simple act of
preparation just because of tradition, rules, or the
fashion of the hour.

Why did David choose five stones when only one
was needed to defeat the giant? Since we were children, the story of this small boy facing Goliath with
what to us is a simple toy and a few rocks has fas-
cinated us. Surely David demonstrated astronomical

faith against insurmountible odds. But wait! A careful study reveals the fact that even though his trust in the Lord was immense, this lad had spent all his young life acquiring the skill necessary to effectively use this deadly weapon. In this biblical situation, it is clearly evident that God was on the side of the army with the heaviest artillery—David's faith coupled with a slingshot and stones.

Once David had his feet firmly planted and that deadly sling was swinging through the air, Goliath was finished! This shepherd boy could probably split a hair with his right or left hand at forty feet. When the rock left the sling, it traveled at the rate of approximately 200 feet per second and delivered a thrust of about 500 foot-pounds. Incidentally, this compares with the power of a derringer or even that of a Colt .45.

But we still have not answered the question, Why five stones? I think that David's computerlike mind was saying, "I have killed the lion and the bear. I do not think that a giant's skull is any thicker. But if one stone doesn't stop him, I will have time for four others. The first shot I'll put in the temple. If that just slows him down, I'll shoot one in each ear. Then I'll have one left for each eye. If he keeps coming after all those stones, I'm finished!"

Why five stones? Those rocks illustrate the *humility* of David. We have the idea that a champion says, "Oh, I'm not very good." That is false humility. Humility is knowing that, "I am a champion. But without the Lord, that's all I am."

In "the valley of the shadow of death," David used all of his resources and abilities. Indeed, the Lord is with us during difficult days and in trying circumstances, but he expects us to use the gifts and available supplies which are ours.

When we commit ourselves to the Lord and he becomes our shepherd, nothing can harm us. Does this seem to be a foolish statement? Are you thinking, "Wait a minute. Nobody ever gets beyond the reach of trouble."

That is exactly correct! No life is strong enough to be immune from trouble. You cannot escape trouble through fantasy or by denying its reality. You cannot avoid it by using drugs or alcohol. Trouble is a part of the givenness of life.

Some people do not accept the existence of trouble. We see it in their prayers: "Why should this happen to me? What have I done to deserve this?" The book of Job destroyed the theological notion that the good do not suffer while the evil always do. The idea that God watches over the righteous and visits disaster on evil men just does not measure up to the facts of life.

We do not find such teaching in Psalm 23. The psalmist did not write, "I will *meet* no evil." He said, "I will *fear* no evil: [Evil will come, but I will not fear it] for thou art with me." It is in this high and lofty relationship with God that the shepherd affirmed he was beyond the reach of trouble. Every tunnel has light at both ends.

Fear is a real problem which we face. This emotion goes far back in human history. It has many diverse forms and belies itself in disguised aspects of personality. Nobody completely escapes it. A psychiatrist wrote, "If fear were abolished from modern life, the work of the psychotherapist would be almost gone."

We hear plenty about sin, but the church is almost completely silent concerning fear. This was not true of Jesus. He did say, "Go, and sin no more," (John 8:11). But he also said, "Fear not." "Be not afraid." "Be not anxious."

Fear drains strength from us. It depletes our resources. It strangles the spirit from life. It imprisons us. Fear paralyzes life. We use the expression: "He was scared stiff" or "He was scared to death." Our phobias come in numerous varieties: fear of others, fear of ourselves, fear of change, fear of height, fear of enclosed places, fear of growing old, fear of disease, fear of poverty. Fear is an emotion of extremely high velocity and voltage.

The fact that the Lord is your shepherd helps alleviate fear. To keep company with him, you have to live a life that is clean and upright. A life free of fear must be such a life.

In the Garden of Eden, Adam discovered what people have found to be true through the years: As soon as the first man had eaten the forbidden fruit, he said to God, "I was afraid, . . . and I hid myself" (Gen.

3:10). Does that sound familiar? "I was afraid. I hid."
We sin. Conscience begins to knock on our door.
Guilt enters into our lives and festers within us. We
sin again, and suddenly we have a habit on our
hands. Sin comes dressed in the garments of so-
called freedom, but this freedom actually is tyranny.
We are free to start, but we are not free to stop. One
fear arrives with a whole army of other fears that
eventually disintegrate life.

To be free from fear, a person must live an upright
life. If you have this kind of life, do not lose it. If you
have lost this kind of life, recover it. Nothing is as
effective to take fear from your life as the awareness
deep within of the shepherd's nearness. "I will fear
no evil: for thou art with me."

I hear many people talking about wanting to be on
"higher ground with God," to climb above the low-
lands of life. Do you have a desire for a more intimate walk with the Lord? We speak about
mountaintop experiences, and we envy those who
have climbed the heights. So often we have the
wrong idea of how this fellowship occurs. We imagine that these people are airlifted to higher ground.

However, we go to higher ground just as ordinary
sheep go. There is only one way there—by climbing
up through the valleys, not *down* through the valleys. Every mountain has its valley, and the best way
to the top is always through the valley.

Dr. Richard Hudson tells of visiting Scotland with
a friend. Sometimes they rode bicycles or traveled on

horseback, but most of the time they walked. One day they came to a picturesque inn on a lake where they spent the night.

The following day they were talking to the inn-keeper concerning the trail they should take as they continued their journey. "You are three or four miles from the most beautiful lake in Scotland," the innkeeper said, "Lake Lochy."

"Tell us how to get there," Hudson requested. Soon their new friend had given directions for a long, roundabout route.

"Isn't there a closer way?"

"Yes, you can go down through the valley," the innkeeper said. "We call it 'the dark mile'! The trail extends through a deep gorge. It is a dark, gloomy place. The vegetation is pale and water drips from the frightening, overhanging cliffs. No one goes through 'the dark mile' unless there is no alterna-tive."

Needless to say, Dr. Hudson and his friend took the nearest route. In the middle of the valley, there were tremendous walls of rock on both sides of the tiny path. It was so dark that, as they looked up, they could see the stars. They continued walking through that damp, forbidding place.

Suddenly, they came out on a little ridge overlook-ing magnificent Lake Lochy. Hudson and his com-panion gasped. They would never forget the sight. The friend remarked, "You know, if we had not walked through 'the dark mile,' I don't believe that we would have appreciated the beauty of Lake Lochy."

Through the dark mile, "the valley of the shadow," God calls us deeper into life. The word I emphasize is *through*. Sometimes there is no alternate path; sometimes we must go *through* the dark mile—with the promise of God that we *will* go "through" it.

In this verse, the psalmist was referring to the dark valley of death. However, to the Christian, even the valley of death becomes a tunnel with light at both ends. At every memorial service for those who know Christ, I read Psalm 23, and I remind those in attendance that the most important word of comfort found in the Psalm is the word *through*. The psalmist said, "Yea, though I walk *through*." This is the victory that Christ gives to those who know him as Shepherd and Lord.

Why does the shepherd lead the sheep to the higher ground by going through the valleys? That is the easiest and gentlest means of arriving at the high places. The sheep could not climb the sheer cliffs. Going through the valley assures the shepherd of water and nourishment.

There are dangers in the valley. A mudslide or a sudden hailstorm can wipe out a whole flock of sheep. Yet, the shepherd knows that going through the valley is worth the risk. As God leads us through difficult situations, we must remember that these valleys lead us upward. We find refreshment with the Lord and encouragement for others who follow.

All of us understand what it means to be in a valley. Those who have gone down in the valley with the Lord know that danger is there. But only by going through the valley can we finally reach the high country. Thorns may rip us, predators may attack, the rivers may overwhelm and threaten to drown us; but because God is in the situation with us, we "shall not fear." To live like this means that we have taken some long steps toward the high country of holy, calm, healthy living with the Shepherd.

The miracle of this Scripture is that the psalmist did not ask to escape the shadow of death. The psalmist did not even ask that he not be afraid. Instead, he affirmed that he would not be afraid; and then he wrote one of the greatest truths of the world: God will be there too. The presence of God was the secret of the psalmist's fearlessness. Death cannot be evaded, but "I will fear no evil: for thou art with me." Here David was not writing about a person; he was talking to a person: "Thou art with me."

A soldier asked his commanding officer if he could go to no-man's-land between the trenches to bring back one of his buddies who lay seriously wounded.

"You may go," said the officer, "but it's too late. It's not worth the risk. Your friend is probably dead, and you will throw your own life away."

But the soldier went. Somehow he managed to reach his friend, lift him on his shoulder, and bring him to safety. The two of them tumbled together and lay in the bottom of the trench.

The officer looked tenderly at the rescuer and said, "I told you it wouldn't be worth it. Your friend is dead, and you are critically wounded."

"It was worth it, Sir."

"How do you mean, worth it? I tell you, your friend is dead."

"Yes, Sir," the hero answered. "But it was worth it because when I got to him he said, 'I knew you'd come.'" The soldier did not save his friend from the shadowed experience, but he altered the effect of the experience.

Is Jesus your Lord? Is he your Shepherd? Do you know this because of a personal experience with him? If he is, then you have already discovered that in every valley, as with every tunnel, there is a light at both ends.

6

The Lord's Gentle Prod

"Thy rod and thy staff they comfort me" (Ps. 23:4).

From our earliest recollections, stories from the Scriptures which we heard at church gave us visual images that were quite unlike the truths of the passages. The teacher of a first-grade class asked the youngsters to illustrate the twenty-third Psalm. After they read the chapter carefully, each child chose a phrase and diligently began his work.

Several students molded shepherds with their sheep from stiff, homemade clay. Some splashed tempera paint on brown paper and outlined small streams, deep valleys—those are part of "the house of the Lord." The remainder of the boys and girls chose plain pieces of paper from the ample supply and drew scenes with felt-tipped watercolor pens.

At the conclusion of the hour, the teacher let the children tell about their masterpieces. Most of the art work was easily identified. However, one picture puzzled even this long-time worker.

Jimmy's scene depicted a man in a brown suit and tie seated behind a huge desk. All around were men and women, standing as though they were listening to his every word. He explained, "This is Rod and his staff."

In fact, the rod and staff were integral parts of the shepherd's attire and possessions. His headdress was usually a handkerchief which fell over his neck and was bound to his head by finger-thick ropes made of camel's hair. His body was covered with an unbleached shirt, gathered at the waist by a leather belt. In cold weather, the shepherd wore a thick, warm, sleeveless camel's hair garment. It was usually striped with shades of brown.

John the Baptist, who many believe was originally a shepherd, wore a shepherd's outer coat of camel's hair. As described in the Bible, his clothing showed that he did not wear the rich robes of the priest but the lowly dress of a layman, a shepherd.

Attached to the leather belt of the shepherd was his purse, a fact which is mentioned several times in the New Testament. Also, he carried a knife and a club. The club was called a *rod*. It was a little over two feet long with a knob at one end. Usually, iron nails were driven into the end of the rod to give it extra weight and force. A noose ran through the handle end so that the rod could be attached to the belt. When in action, this noose was wrapped around the wrist to prevent the rod from being dropped or struck from the shepherd's hand.

Every shepherd boy spent hours practicing with the rod and learning how to throw it with amazing speed and confident accuracy. This club was the main weapon used in defense for himself and his sheep. It was the symbol of his strength, power, and authority as a shepherd.

The term *rod* crept into the colloquial language of the West. *Rod* is a slang term applied to handguns, such as pistols and revolvers, which are carried by cowboys in Western movies. The connotation is exactly the same as used in this Psalm. The shepherd's rod was his weapon of power.

Remember when God called Moses, the desert shepherd, and sent him to deliver Israel from Egypt's bondage? The rod was used to demonstrate Moses' power and authority. It was always through Moses' rod that miracles were accomplished to convince Pharaoh of Moses' divine commission and to give confidence to the people of Israel. The rod represented God's mind and will. It implied authority and carried with it the convincing power and the impact of the Old Testament terminology: "Thus saith the Lord."

There was comfort in seeing the rod in the shepherd's hand. In our day there should be assurance in our hearts as we see the authority of God's Word. For the Scriptures are God's rod, an extension of his mind, will, and intentions.

The Associated Press carried the story of a man who lived in this country illegally for thirty years.

The immigration authorities discovered the fact and took steps to deport him. Digging into the case, they found themselves confronted with an unusual international dilemma. The alien stood before officials, waving his arms, and in his broken English tried to tell them that they could not deport him. The small country in Central Europe in which he was born no longer existed. Because of the shifting of boundaries after the war, his country was wiped out.

A similar experience has happened to all of us. The land of our birth, the land of our childhood, is not here anymore. We live in a different world where numerous confusing voices and strange philosophies are presented. Society today has a so-called code of morals which is not moral at all; it is absolutely immoral! If we are to experience the Christian life of joy, we must regularly and systematically turn to the Word of God and discover in its pages the Shepherd's hand of authority. This exacting, clean-cut, powerful instrument is the only weapon which we can use to keep out confusion amid chaos. Thus the psalmist wrote: "Thy rod . . . comforts me."

The shepherd used the rod for discipline or warning. If he observed a sheep wandering away, approaching poisonous weeds, or getting too close to danger, the rod would go whistling through the air, sending the wayward animal rushing back to the flock.

Around the turn of the century, a fire chief in San Francisco went to the city council. "Gentlemen," he said, "you have made a serious mistake. The main line of the water supply for this city passes over the Saint Andreas fault." This brilliant man explained that if the city ever had a major earthquake, it would occur at the Saint Andreas fault and that the water-line would be severed. "There will be no way for us to extinguish all the fires which would sweep the city." The council heard the plea, and they understood the rationale of the chief. But because of other matters, they tabled this problem to consider at a later date.

Several years passed. In 1906, an earthquake shook San Francisco; and the waterline was broken. The uncontrollable fire which ensued snuffed out the lives of nearly seven hundred people. Four-fifths of the city was leveled because water was not available to stop the catastrophe. The fire chief who had issued the warning was killed in the fire as his home collapsed at the first impact of the earthquake.

How many times God has admonished us about the wages of sin! How often in our study of the Scriptures have we been impressed with the fact that the Spirit of God was calling us back to the point of beginning again with him? The Word of God comes to our hearts with surprising suddenness for correction and reproof when we tend to go astray.

The shepherd's rod was also employed for counting the sheep. In the Old Testament we read of passing under the rod (Lev. 27:32). When a sheep passed under the rod, it had been counted and examined with great care. A sheep externally might look all right; but because of its long wool, some disease could be hidden from the shepherd.

Psalm 139 says, "Search me, O God, and know my heart: try me, and know my thoughts: And see if there be any wicked way in me" (v. 23). Is God searching your life? If so, what is he finding? As he touches areas of your life, be sensitive to God's leadership. Being convicted of wrong is not enough. Having the wool pushed aside and the disease diagnosed is not a cure. Drastic steps must be taken to remove the sin, to heal the infection or weakness.

"Thy rod and thy staff they comfort me." The staff which the shepherd carried was like a scoutpole. About six or eight feet in length, it had a multitude of uses. Shepherds often had refreshing naps while leaning on the top of the staff. It is interesting to observe that the word *bridge* does not appear even one time in the Bible. The streams were crossed in the rainy season by putting the staff in the middle of the stream and leaping to the other side.

More than any other item, the staff identified the shepherd. In no other profession was the shepherd's staff carried. It was uniquely an instrument used in the care and management of sheep—designed, shaped, and adapted especially for their needs. A symbol of concern, it signified the compassion which the shepherd had for his sheep.

The staff was extended to catch individual sheep, young or old, and draw them close to the shepherd

for examination. It was most useful for the shy and
timid sheep which usually stayed away from the
shepherd. With it he brought them back into the
flock and to himself. The staff was helpful in direct-
ing and guiding the flock. It was employed to direct
them onto a new path or to push them through a gate
or through a long, difficult route. The shepherd
would lay the tip of the stick gently against the animal's side, apply pressure, and steer the sheep in the
way he wanted it to go.

Can you picture a shepherd using his staff to gently guide his sheep? This certainly must have given
assurance to these animals. The Holy Spirit per-
forms exactly the same function in our lives. He fills
our lives and seeks to make us more like Jesus.

E. Stanley Jones was lost once in the jungles of
India and secured a native from the area to guide
him back to civilization. For many hours the man cut
through the bush. Being ignorant of the jungle, Dr.
Jones asked, "Where is the path?"

The guide glanced at him and replied, "Sir, I am
the path." This is what Jesus affirms, "I am the way.
I am the path."

Many times in our pilgrimage, we face decisions
which are totally confusing. When the Spirit of God
has been making us like Jesus, the mind of the Good
Shepherd is within us, and he becomes the way.

When I first became a Christian, this new life
seemed easy. From my point of view, being baptized
and being a church member required no effort at all.

In fact, it was fun! My parents were proud of me, all my aunts and uncles remarked how sweet I was, and the adults in the church told me I was a fine boy.

I recall the time, a few years later, when my Sunday School teacher taught me the type of life a Christian is to follow. He reminded me about the rules which the Scriptures teach. I thought, "Being a Christian is tough! It will be hard to measure up to this standard. I'm not sure that I can!"

Then my pastor helped me see the full claims of God on my life. He pointed out some extremely difficult commands of our Lord. Why, this new insight revealed that being a Christian on my own will and strength is impossible! I could never please God!

Tragically, many young Christians stop right there. Their development ceases completely. They become overwhelmed with the demands of Jesus Christ on their lives. "I can never make it," they state, with remorse.

I moved from stage 1: *It's easy!* to stage 2: *It's hard!* to stage 3: *It's impossible!* to stage 4: *It's exciting!* Stage 4 is very important. If we are to grow in our Christian pilgrimage, this step is vital. Without the enabling and empowering of the Holy Spirit, stagnation occurs. When the Holy Spirit fills my life, I have the strength and capacity to become the person God intended. When the Holy Spirit fills any life, the Christian walk becomes exciting!

We cannot fulfill the demands of Jesus Christ without a daily infilling. When we sincerely desire his guidance and ask him to control our lives, he gives us more of life than we ever dreamed possible.

The Christian life experiences firsthand the feel of God's touch, the sense of the Holy Spirit. For the child of God, there is an intimate, subtle, yet magnificent sense of the Comforter at his side. This verse leaves this impression, "Trust the Good Shepherd, and you will be comforted."

In the comic strip, "Peanuts," many times we have seen Charlie Brown and Lucy with a football. How funny some of those incidents have been! In one cartoon, Charlie is quite certain that Lucy's offer to hold the ball for his placekick will end up as all the other attempts have. She will pull the ball away exactly as he is ready to kick it. His foot will go into the air, and he will end up flat on his back. He said to her: "You must think I'm crazy. You say you'll hold the ball, but you won't. You'll pull it away like you always have, and I'll break my neck."

With a heavenly look, Lucy responded, "Why, Charlie Brown, how you talk! I wouldn't think of such a thing. I'm a changed person. Look. Isn't this a face you can trust?"

And since Charlie Brown is Charlie Brown, he accepts Lucy at her word. "All right, you hold the ball; and I'll come running up and kick it."

Sure enough, the expected happens; and he flies through the air and smashes to the ground. He can only wail, "She did it again."

In the last scene, a properly penitent Lucy leans

over Charlie and chortles, "I admire you, Charlie
Brown. You have such great faith in human nature."

Because there are numerous Lucys in the world,
many people tragically do not trust anybody. They
do not trust themselves. Therefore, they do not think
anybody else is trustworthy. Some live by Abe Lin-
coln's observation: "You can fool all the people some
of the time and some of the people all the time."

The whole story of mankind is a history of persons
not keeping faith with others. Wars have been
started, businesses have failed, marriages have been
destroyed, families have been shattered, and people
have been proven deficient because one or another in
a relationship did not keep trust alive and well.

As a nation, we desperately need to trust in God.
Our coins read, "IN GOD WE TRUST." That is exactly what we must do again. Then we need to trust
completely the members of our family and those who
are within the framework of the church. Officials
who have been elected to high office should have our
complete support until their corruption and immo-
rality have been proven beyond the shadow of a
doubt. We must restore confidence in our society by
being Christians who are almost naive in simplicity
compared to the standards of the world. By trusting
people who come begging and exploiting, let us pray
that they will see in us the possibility of what they
can become.

No, I am not referring to ignorant trust. That is
not a solution. Anyone who blindly depends on an-

other and who believes in him without being conscious of that person's flaws, imperfections, and limitations will certainly be the victim of tragedy! I am talking about a basic trust in the Good Shepherd, a personal relationship with Jesus Christ, which includes a plan of love, acceptance, and brotherhood—the genius of God's kingdom in this world.

Because of overwhelming evil today, many people are afraid. Sometimes all of us feel helpless—and we are until we find comfort in realizing that God's hand and power are involved in history. "Thy rod and thy staff, they comfort me." That's good news!

7

Inexhaustible
Provisions

"Thou preparest a table before me in the presence of mine enemies: thou anointest my head with oil; my cup runneth over" (Ps. 23:5).

Early in the spring, perhaps before all the snow had melted, the shepherd surveyed the rough mountain ranges for new grazing land. In Texas we call areas of this kind *mesas* or high, summer ranges. The loving shepherd examined these tablelands with infinite care. He expended much time and effort as he prepared for the arrival of the sheep since he desired the best of everything for his flock during the summer months.

Immediately before the sheep came into the high altitudes, the shepherd made another journey and completed the preparation for their arrival. He distributed salt and minerals at strategic locations. He took care in finding campsites so that the sheep would have the best possible bed-grounds. As the shepherd decided how long different tablelands

89

could be used for grazing, he also checked the ground for poisonous weeds and planned his grazing program to avoid them or took drastic steps to remove them.

These facts were in David's mind when he wrote the words of this Scripture. I can see the shepherd boy walking over the summer range ahead of his flock. His sharp eyes looked for any sign of poisonous plants, which he pulled from the ground.

The Christian application is clear. Like sheep, we try everything that comes along. Many people believe they have not lived until they have tasted this, until they have sampled that, just to see what it is like. And so, trouble comes. The problem is that some things are deadly.

We can avoid severe grief and hardship by recalling that our Master has gone before us, grappling with every situation which would otherwise overcome us. Recall the time Jesus warned Peter of the temptation which was to follow. Jesus knew temptation and the strength and power necessary to resist the forces of evil. He gives us the ability to be "more than conquerors" (Rom. 8:37) if we will only use it.

As Christians, we must be about the business of seeking to have a climate in our cities and communities where children will not be confronted with so many overt temptations. My three boys have been vaccinated against various diseases, and I am thankful to medical science for going ahead of my children to prevent or destroy the cause of the disease. Parents, scientists, governments, and society must join together in preparing the table, the community, so that all good life may be safely nourished. One way to do this is to disapprove of and avoid some television programs and movies.

In the world today, the church must serve as the shepherd who makes preparation for the sheep. With violence and evil masquerading as the only way of life, the body of believers has an obligation to join together and to help our communities return to basic Christian principles.

The oldest living things, the giant sequoias of the California mountains provide an excellent parallel for the church. These massive trees always grow exactly perpendicular. They develop in total harmony with the pull of gravity. If the tree tilts for any reason, it rapidly grows a compensating root. This new support pulls it back in line.

A type of acid is found in the sequoia bark which boring worms cannot tolerate. So these pests, which usually prove deadly to such vegetation, are eliminated as a threat. Sequoias also contain tremendous healing properties. If lightning strikes, every resource of the tree speeds to the burned area. Immediately, a swift restoring process begins. These ancient giants always grow in clumps. Their roots are so intertwined that a strong wind could not uproot a single tree. Sequoias stand strong.

Regardless of the external attacks of the enemy, the true family of God will stand intact. The church has within her power the ability to grow straight and tall, reaching toward the Lord while sending roots deep into his nourishing Word. Love, harmony, and prayer are a few of the elements which are repulsive to the church's enemies.

The church must seek to restore those members who are injured. She must outlive the sometime accurate criticism that "the Christian army is the only army in the world that shoots its wounded." Finally, as the members bind themselves together with Jesus Christ as their Source of life, they are able to withstand any onslaught.

"Thou preparest a table before me." Now the word *table* may simply stand for a meal. However, *table* means more than just an indoor banquet. In another psalm we read, "Can God furnish a table in the wilderness?" (Ps. 78:19) The literal meaning of the word is "something spread out." So, in this verse two meanings are implied: "The flat place of the grass" and "plenty to eat."

Not only did the shepherd have to prepare the tableland high in the mountains but also he had to conquer other enemies of the sheep. He found and destroyed the deadly cobra. But the most dangerous enemy was the eighteen-inch horned viper, which was easily overlooked. If the shepherd saw one of these lethal creatures, he tried to kill it; for vipers would bite the noses of the sheep as they grazed. These vicious enemies were one of the main reasons the shepherds led the sheep instead of driving them.

Shepherds were constantly looking for horned vipers and eliminating them from the path of the flock.

Jesus goes ahead of us, his sheep, not only in temptation but also in life situations. He has already experienced every extremity which we face. We know from history that he entered completely and intimately into the lives of men upon earth. He has known our sufferings, experienced our sorrows, endured our struggles. He was a man of sorrows and acquainted with grief. He identified thoroughly with us. Therefore, we can never look at him and say, "But, you don't understand!" because we are in the control of Christ, who has prepared the table for us.

With poisonous plants, predators, vipers, and other wild animals all around, it was imperative for the sheep or lambs to walk close to the shepherd. The wandering sheep, the sheep fartherest from the shepherd, slips off and is destroyed in an unsuspecting moment. Those who walk with Jesus, the Good Shepherd, go through life confident and secure. Here is the secure place in the midst of this troubled world.

Wait. There is more. "Thou preparest a table before me in the presence of mine enemies: thou anointest my head with oil; my cup runneth over." Picture the sheep in the high meadowland where there are clear, clean, running springs. The grass is fresh and tender, and there is daily contact with the shepherd. But it is summertime, the season which brings all the parasites that so trouble sheep: the warble flies, botflies, heel flies, ear flies, blackflies, mosquitoes, gnats, and other winged parasites. Their attacks on sheep can turn these peaceful months into times of physical torture for the flock.

At the end of the day, the shepherd would stand in the gateway, call the sheep to the fold, and examine them individually. In addition to the flies and parasites, the shepherd knew that the sheep were subject to fevers. Their feet might need attention; a scratched head or a torn knee should be soothed by the shepherd's oil. Water in a large two-handed cup was at the shepherd's feet. Sometimes the trickling stream was so rerouted that it flowed into the cup and out again.

Always, "my cup runneth over." This statement gives evidence of the abundance which is found with the shepherd at the sheepfold. Sheep are nervous when drinking water at a running stream. They are instinctively terrified because their wool renders them easily liable to be carried away. As we have discovered previously, sheep will not drink at a swiftly-flowing stream. I am told that when a sheepfold is built near the Jordan River, the water is routed into backwater so that it will be calm.

In the Holy Land, streams are volatile. At one period of the year, there is ample water—to the flood stage. During another period, water is scarce and precious. Moving water must be put into some kind of container so the sheep can drink without fear from a receptacle that is brimming and overflowing.

This is the expressive picture behind these words: "Thou anointest my head with oil; my cup runneth over."

The inhabitants of Palestine were noted for their hospitality. A stranger was welcome at any meal. As the host entertained his guest, he engaged him in conversation and then determined whether they were compatible in personality and interest. If, in the course of a meal a friendship developed, the host, while filling the cup of his guest, purposely filled the cup to the brim and allowed some to overflow. This was an overt sign that the stranger could come into this household for a visit of any length and that true friendship had been established.

Is this not what our Lord is teaching here? If he is our Shepherd, our lives, bound to him in a relationship of love, are overflowing. He has a cup which is filled beyond capacity, waiting for all who accept his friendship.

In Palestine today there are some large sheepfolds. Sometimes several shepherds will put their flocks together for protection. At dawn it is thrilling to see the different shepherds separating their flocks by calling or playing a pipe. The sheep go with their particular shepherd; there seems to be no confusion in this process. In the dilemmas of this life, how we need to remember that the Good Shepherd gave his life for us so we might follow his voice.

When tragedy comes and when it is hard to believe that God loves us, we should be comforted by know-

ing that the Lord does not desire our crisis. He does
not hand out cancer to one and bankruptcy to another, not sorrow to some and frustration and mental
disorder to others. God allows these crises in our
lives to serve as discipline if we react properly.

"I am the door of the sheep . . . . by me, if any man
enter in, he shall be saved" (John 10:7, 9). When all
the sheep had passed into the fold, the shepherd
built a fire at the gate. Over this fire he cooked his
food, then wrapped himself in his warm outer cloak,
and fell asleep. The lion and the bear, which were
prevalent in those days, could reach the sheep only
through that gateway. At the gate was the fire and
body of the shepherd.

How the empty, lonely, and fearful need the Shepherd who is like this! Are you looking for security?
The Good Shepherd specializes in seeking the disen-
franchised, the lost. The sheep within the fold can
hear the wolf, but between the sheep and complete
destruction are high walls and thorns, the fire, and
above everything else, the body, the very life, of the
Shepherd.

When we get bruised and cut and are victims of
the "vipers" in this world, the Good Shepherd always comes with the balm of Gilead—with the oil
and the cup to restore us, to position us once again
in his will.

The return of H. C. Morrison to this country following a lifetime of missionary service in China is a
moving story. It so happened that he was coming to

the United States on the same ship which carried Teddy Roosevelt. The president had been on a safari in Africa. As the ship passed Sandy Hook and came toward New York harbor, there were signs of welcome all around. Barges floated out with blaring bands; flags, banners, and streamers were everywhere in sight. Firefighting boats sprayed their welcome to the sky.

Morrison realized that all of this fanfare was for the president returning from a holiday. Morrison then fell into the grip of self-pity. He knew that no one would be meeting him at the dock. Then he recalled what he had tried to do in China and thought how little anyone cared. As he folded his hands and leaned on the deck rail, feeling sorry for himself, Missionary Morrison said he heard a voice come to him like the sound of many waters. It said, "But you are not home yet!"

I thought of the verse, "They have their reward" (Matt. 6:2). In this life we may not see all the crooked ways being made straight. But this life is only a glimpse, just a beginning, of a pilgrimage for those who intimately know the Good Shepherd. It is easy to develop the habit of being negative when our attention is fixed on the things of this earth. A boy found a brand new dime. He resolved to watch the ground wherever he went for the rest of his life in the hope of finding more coins. As a result he acquired a permanent stoop, weak lungs, nearsightedness, no friends, and $29.89!

When we always look down, we miss the grandeur and the beauty of the mountains and the stars. God seems to indicate that there will be sheep in every flock which spend all their time looking down, while some sheep spend their time looking up at the Shepherd. Those who look to Jesus are discovering an overflowing life.

Are you living in his tableland?

8

On Our Trail: Goodness and Mercy

"Surely goodness and mercy shall follow me all the days of my life" (Ps. 23:6).

In the musical, *South Pacific,* Mary Martin sang a song with a catchy tune and almost unforgettable words. "I'm stuck like a dope with a thing called hope and I can't get it out of my heart!"

Some scholars believe that the psalmist had this same idea in mind when he wrote, "Surely goodness and mercy shall follow me all the days of my life." I do not accept this concept! He did not write, "I *hope for* goodness and mercy." He did not write, "I am *planning on* goodness and mercy." With confidence he stated, "Surely [surely, surely, *I'm positive*] goodness and mercy shall follow me all the days of my life."

David was an old man when he wrote this incisive psalm. He had experienced tragedy and disappointment, but in the process, he had come to acknowledge the Lord as Shepherd. He had discovered God

101

to be someone who can restore life and can remove fear. In spite of the dark clouds, David felt that with his Lord, the sun would shine tomorrow! He was presumptuous about the coming days.

We are skilled in thinking ourselves into disaster. We feel bad, and we fill our minds with thoughts of being sick. Beginning the day dreading that something terrible is going to happen, we then look to tomorrow with fear and trembling.

A young man approached the bus stop where he awaited his crosstown transportation every afternoon. Of an older gentleman who was propped against the lamp pole as though he were supporting it, the young man asked, "Hey, Buddy, got a light?" The man stared ahead in icy silence.

Once again the question was raised, "Do you have a match?" Not a sound came from the expressionless figure.

By this time a note of exasperation was evident. "Look, all I want is a light! Why don't you answer me?!"

The man turned slowly and spoke. "Now, let's say that I gave you a light. You would thank me, and we would engage in some small talk about the weather and the traffic problem and the fact that the bus is late.

"Then you would suggest that we go into this cafe and get a cup of coffee. As we talked, we'd realize that we held several interests in common. By then, I'd begin to like you; and so, I would invite you to join my family for dinner on Friday night. Being the friendly sort which you are, you would accept the invitation and come to my house.

"During the course of the evening you'd meet my daughter. You'd ask her out, and later you two would fall in love and would get married. Then you'd have a house full of children. With my luck you'd get sick and die, and I would have to rear your children. I hate kids. That's the reason I won't give you a light!"

This gloomy tale of woe may be an exaggeration, but tragically many refrain from offering friendship because of the cost. The psalmist had good news at this point. He said, "Surely goodness and mercy shall follow me all the days of my life." This verse has a message to Christians. It also speaks to non-Christians and whose lives are filled with doubt and confusion about God and life. It has meaning for those who are trying to resign from life.

Psalm 23 emphasizes the care taken by the loving Shepherd. In this verse the sheep is saying with assurance that good things will happen all the days of his life because of the nature and character of the Shepherd. A sheep with such a Shepherd knows that he is in a privileged position. "I have this kind of shepherd; therefore, goodness and mercy will be the treatment I will always receive." Now, that is a bold statement. In fact, it is a boast! It explains the confidence which this sheep has in the Shepherd who controls his destiny, his life.

Paul said, "And we know that all things work

together for good to them that love God, to them who
are the called according to his purpose" (Rom. 8:28).
Do you believe that? Do you know that no matter
what happens to you the event will be followed by
goodness and mercy?

The title song of a Broadway musical asserts, "On
a clear day you can see forever." My experience is
that only on overcast days do we look thoughtfully
at tomorrow and contemplate forever. If my health
is excellent, my income is flourishing, my family is
well, and my friends all like me, I can easily testify,
"Surely goodness and mercy shall follow me all the
days of my life."

What happens when my body breaks down? What
do I say when I stand helplessly, as I have had to do,
and watch someone I deeply love die slowly? What is
my response when the job folds and suddenly there
is no money to meet the bills? What happens when
my teenagers are "running around with the wrong
crowd"? What do I say when suddenly, without
warning or good reason, friends let me down?

In my life I can look back on experiences which
seemed to predict total calamity. My heart was broken. I cried myself to sleep at night. I wondered why
the Shepherd led me down this blind alley. There
were days which were as dark as the deepest mid-
night. I remember the pain and anguish and realize
that all this trauma turned out for my benefit and
well-being.

If you have walked with the Shepherd for awhile,

you have already discovered that when you are in his care no difficulty can arise and no sin can defeat. When sin enters our lives, we notice immediately that something is missing. A legend tells that the devil was once asked what he missed after his fall from heaven. His answer: "The sound of the trumpets in the morning!!"

I love God because he first loved me. His goodness and mercy is fresh every day. My trust is in him, the Good Shepherd, because I know he loves me. He loves me because he is my "Abba, Father." He is my Shepherd. He forgives; he restores.

The constant flowing of God's life into the believer can cause a situation which resembles the Dead Sea if care is not taken. Even a mineral-rich body of water becomes stagnant, losing its capacity to support life, when it receives and never gives. The Lord intends for his children to be channels through which goodness and mercy outpour into the lives of others.

Sheep have the capacity of being the most ruinous of all beasts. Some foolishly believe that these animals can get along anywhere, but the opposite is true. No other livestock requires more careful handling or personalized attention. Sheep must be under constant, scrupulous watch. They are creatures of habit. When left by themselves, sheep will follow the same old trails until they become ruts; sheep will feed the same hills until they turn to desert. Sheep pollute their own ground until it grows corrupt with disease and parasites. Many of the world's finest sheep ranges have been ruined beyond repair by overgrazing, poor management, and indifferent or ignorant sheep owners. Parts of New Zealand and Australia, areas in the Western United States, as well as in Mesopotamia, Spain, and Greece lie in desolation.

On the other hand, sheep can be the best animals to be placed on eroding acreage. The waste from the body of domestic sheep enriches the soil. Sheep have the habit of sleeping on the higher parts of the pasture and grazing on the lower areas. The rains wash the loose soil and nourishment from the highest terrain into the more productive places. Also, sheep will rid a field of many weeds. These plants are the flock's favorite food. They especially delight in the Canadian thistle, vegetation which will overtake the land if left unchecked. The sheep leave a legacy. When these animals no longer graze an area, if they had proper guidance, the land will be in a better condition than it was previously.

Two men stayed overnight with a family. A couple of days later, one discovered that his hat was missing. He wrote a note to the family: "I think I left my hat at your house. Would you please kindly check and see?" By return mail, he received this reply: "We've searched all over the house, high and low. Your hat cannot be found. The only thing you left behind was a blessing." What a compliment! When we return home after a visit, can our host make such a statement? Or will he exclaim, "Finally, they're gone!"

In Africa today there are markers in numerous places which read, "David Livingstone was Here." Natives, whose language this great doctor never learned, talk about the kindly physician who lovingly cared for them. Everywhere he went, he left marks of goodness and mercy. An often-repeated statement concerning Jesus is, "He went about doing good" (Acts 10:38). We learn from the life of the Savior, from the deeds of a caring missionary, from a little story, and from the habits of sheep that those enriching qualities are to be spent for others.

"Surely goodness and mercy shall follow me all the days of my life." In addition to encouragement for Christians, this verse also contains a clear-cut message to those who do not know Jesus Christ as the Good Shepherd. The sheep were led by the shepherd from one pasture to another. There followed after the dogs of which Job speaks. (Job 30:1) The ever-seeking, always-caring God portrayed in the dramatic story of Job gave Francis Thompson the inspiration to write the poem entitled, "The Hound of Heaven."

This classic depicts a man running from God night and day, across the years, and through the maze of his confused mind. He speaks of hiding from the Lord in tears and laughter. In this poem, one of the greatest truths of God is clearly expressed. God not

only goes before us to lead us, but he is also ceaseless-
ly behind us. Ours is a seeking God.

This same thought is seen in the Bible from Gene-
sis to the Gospels through Revelation. One of the
first questions in the Bible is, "Adam, . . . where art
thou?"(Gen. 3:9). Its last word is a divine call to man:
"And the Spirit and the bride say, Come. And let him
that heareth say, Come. And let him that is athirst
come"(Rev. 22:17).

The Bible is the story of a search. In fact, one of the
basic distinctions between philosophy and theology
is at this point. The philosopher searches for God.
The theologian states that God is looking for man. A
person cannot escape from God. How many men in
the Scriptures were found by God while they were
running away? Jonah, Jacob, Elijah, Saul of Tarsus
are only a few. Our God is the Shepherd who will
never let us go.

The Lord asked Adam, "Where art thou?" We
could insert our own names in this question. He is
calling my name and your name. Where are you
today? Do you believe that the Shepherd is distant or
absent? Hard to find, hiding? Are you hiding from
him? Let me share a secret: He is nearer to us than
we are to each other. He is closer to us than our
hands or our feet.

A college student sought a Christian friend for
counsel. He expressed his problem clearly, "I can't
find God."

"What happened?" the friend asked.

Reluctantly, the student related a familiar but tragic story of meeting a girl at a motel and of spending a night—not of anticipated ecstasy, but of guilt and remorse. "Since that night," he confessed, "I can't find God. I've confessed, prayed, and cried, but I still can't experience peace."

"Who do you think you met in that motel?" asked the counselor.

"You mean the girl?" the student responded.

"No," answered the Christian friend.

The counselor opened his Bible to Psalm 139:7–8 and asked the beleaguered young man to read. Struggling with every word, he read, "Whither shall I go from thy spirit? or whither shall I flee from thy presence? If I ascend up into heaven, thou art there: if I make my bed in . . . in . . ." With tears streaming down his face, he could not continue.

His friend took the Bible and completed the verse: " 'If I make my bed in hell, behold, thou art there.' Your problem is not that you cannot find God but that you cannot get away from God!" the counselor explained. Then he led the student to a fresh experience of cleansing and forgiveness through the blood of Jesus Christ.

Even in the depths of sin, the loving Shepherd is present. His goodness and mercy follow us all the days of our lives. An old country preacher who was speaking on Psalm 23 said, "The Lord is my Shepherd, but that ain't all of it. He has his dogs following along behind me. With the Lord, the Shepherd, in

front of my life and with his two collie dogs, Goodness and Mercy, following along behind, even mean,
old, corrupt sinners like us will be led home."

9

Forever Is a Long, Long Time

"And I will dwell in the house of the Lord for ever" (Ps. 23:6).

The flock of sheep had summered at the top of the mountain. They came down as the cold, rain, and sleet forced them to return to the home place. Soon they were safely enfolded. If sheep could think, perhaps each one would have said to himself, "I will dwell in this sheepfold for the rest of my life. Forever, forever, and forever."

Now that is a beautiful picture. And many commentaries compare such a scene with dwelling "in the house of the Lord forever." This interpretation espouses that when we die we will live in heaven in a posture of rest and meditation throughout eternity. Although I see a degree of truth in the idea, to accept this limited view as it stands seems anticlimactic.

If a movie were made concerning Psalm 23, I am sure that the last segment would portray an old,

113

wrinkled shepherd, his face weathered, his eyes
deeply set, with a shaggy beard and long hair. He
would check the last sheep, light the fire, and finally
lie down in the doorway. Then the cameras would
zoom in for a close-up shot of the shepherd. The film
would conclude as the fire died away and the sky
darkened in the distance.

I cannot buy that! As we walk through the pages
of God's Word, we find in this immortal Psalm too
much movement, revelation, and refreshment to end
the scene on such a low note. Quiet, inactive contem-
plation in some nebulous, distant heaven simply
does not match the movement and cadence of this
Shepherd Psalm.

Remember the words of Jesus in John's Gospel: "I
am the door: by me if any man enter in, he shall be
saved." Then the Lord added, "And shall go in and
out, and find pasture" (10:9) There seems to be more
beyond! Although we might want to rest for awhile
after the shocking transition from this life to a life
with God, I do not think inactivity—except for a
strum or two on a golden harp—is heaven.

"I will dwell in the house of the Lord." The He-
brew word used here for *house* is *beth.* However, we
understand this word as if it were *machan,* a building or a place. We first encounter the word *beth* in
Jacob's vision. With rocks for a pillow, he had a
dream as he slept in the wilderness. He remarked
that he was afraid because that was a horrible place.
It was terrifying to Jacob because God was there.

There was no temple, altar, or other marking; but Jacob perceived the presence of God and felt unclean. He named the place Beth-el, "the house of God."

This interpretation of *house* is very similar to the Greek word *oikos* which is used in John 14, "in my Father's house are many mansions" (v.2). House can mean "a building," but also it can be used as "the house of Tudor" or "the house of Windsor." Therefore, this phrase could be rendered "in the house of God." The word for *mansion* should be translated "inn" or "motel." In light of this understanding, we conclude that when death comes, we do not go into a gigantic house, close the door, and live forever. Life in the Father's house includes growth and progression. Jesus called himself "the door" and said that those who were saved would go in and out "and find pasture."

As for Christians in this present life, I imagine that most of us will not go far past the nursery in spiritual matters. Perhaps in heaven, we will have the opportunity to continue growing. However, we must understand a simplistic fact: Unless heaven gets to earth through us while we live, we will never get to heaven when the things of earth pass away!

My dad died several years ago; he graduated from this world to that eternal dwelling place. Some sixteen years prior to this event, he was critically ill. It was necessary for him to go to New Orleans and undergo a new and dangerously complex surgical procedure. The operation entailed the rerouting of his blood, the clamping off of one artery to remove pressure from another place deep in his head.

Medically, he died during the surgery. Through a miracle he survived the ordeal and began a somewhat limited life. Later, he told the family of his experience at this moment of death.

Now, my dad was a hardworking, rather hardnosed, practical sort of person who certainly was not given to visions and dreams. He was a realist, as well as being a new Christian. He accepted Christ late in life and knew little of God and the church.

He told us that at the very moment everyone thought he was gone, he did, in fact, die. "I went to heaven," he said. "But do you know what I was in heaven? A little, bitty baby. All around me was splendor and gold that I can't describe—I can't understand. But I remember being such a little baby. And I wanted to grow, to get bigger. I wondered how in the world could I grow up."

Following Dad's illness, I stayed around only a short while. I was away from home for many years and had very limited contact with my dad, other than in a casual sense. At the time of his death, I discovered that in his latter years he privately studied the Bible.

In our home we always had a family altar. We prayed together and my dad would pray, but he would never get by himself and study. While going through his things in the small country store which he maintained until his death, I found a Bible, marked and worn, with some pages turned down, and a few greasy spots and tear marks on it. Then I realized that my dad, who experienced the traumatic ordeal of going to heaven in his mind, returned as a full, whole person, desiring to grow spiritually. (I know he is in heaven today—still growing!)

In the life and teaching of Jesus, nothing indicates that growth and development cease after death. There is more to come! Even the secular, yet thrilling novel, *Jonathan Livingston Seagull,* speaks of the higher dimension, of more beyond. When we leave this life, we do not join some huge angelic chorus and disappear into oblivion. We are transformed for a fuller fellowship with God in Jesus Christ with greater challenges, responsibilities, and opportunities.

Jesus always wanted to go further. As a boy of twelve, Jesus would have been safer in the caravan with the other youngsters. He was not there. He was in the Temple talking with the doctors. We can imagine that many mornings in Nazareth Mary would go to his bed, and he would be gone. Then she would notice that tousled head coming down from the mountains, where he had been learning more about God. He settled down to business. He found security and prosperity in the carpenter's shop, but the Father had other plans for his only begotten Son. The itinerant Messiah could not be contained in one village. "Get the boat ready." The fields were "white unto harvest."

When Jesus became the sacrificial Lamb, even the tomb could not hold him! His disciples had been scattered all over the world when they died. His overpowering conviction had burned daily in the hearts of the apostles. John died in Ephesus. Peter and Paul died near Rome. James died in Jerusalem. Thomas died in India. Bartholomew died in Armenia.

The life beyond is in another dimension; it is far more marvelous than the mind can comprehend. I have a secret theory. I believe that God did not relate more about heaven because if we understood fully, we would do everything possible to arrive there quickly!

Jesus expects us to grow right now, in every circumstance of life, with him. As children we sang the chorus, "Every day with Jesus Is sweeter than the day before." Is that statement true in your life? "The longer I serve Him, the sweeter He grows."

People have been moving, searching since the dawn of creation. The Aussie preacher, F. W. Boreham, tells a story entitled, "The Other Side of The Hill." His premise is that the oldest question in the world is, "What is on the other side of the hill?" A man is looking to the far horizons in the cool of the evening, gazing at the hilltops as they break the skyline and muttering to himself. *I wonder. I wonder what is on the other side of that mountain.*

Boreham wrote that such inquisitiveness gave rise

to history and geography. In the beginning, man looked out toward the distant hills and wondered. He simply wondered. But his sons and grandsons climbed those hills. They went beyond the hills, east and west, north and south, losing touch with the old home. They climbed one range, then another. They settled in this valley, that valley; and thus tribes, nations, and empires came into existence. This is the quest which sent us into outer space. We went up, and we will go on and on. Why? Because something is there! The other side of the hill—that is what did it! The charm of the unknown and the everlasting whisper deep within call us onward.

Unfortunately, some people never experience the desire for "more beyond." They remain in a self-imposed bondage, refusing to follow guidance or direction. A limited, selfish world is without hope or caring.

The pastures of two sheep ranches were separated by a fence which extended to the sea. One flock was cared for by its owner, a generous, loving man who took every precaution in providing for his sheep. On his side of the fence the grass was lush and green, fresh water was abundant, and the flock was examined often for diseases and wounds.

Across the way a sorry excuse for a shepherd managed the sheep. Those scrawny, sickly animals were the victims of parasites, rough travel, and inadequate diet. The pastures had only a few sprigs of grass clumped sparsely over the rocky ground, not nearly enough to feed them all. Longingly, the flock would stand at the fence and gaze upon the abundant pasture on the other side.

At Christmastime the tides were more radical than ever before. The fence did not extend far out into the sea. Low tide allowed some of the sheep to go around the barrier. The hungry animals would devour the rich, green grass. Because they were not accustomed to such a diet, their digestive systems were overtaxed and many died immediately.

One day the good shepherd found three sheep at the point of death. He picked them up like old sacks, put them into a wheelbarrow, and rolled them around the fence to his neighbor. This unconcerned man took his knife and slit their throats.

The world in which we live is inhabited by the forces of evil. Those who live as though this were the only world are extremely shortsighted. The treasures of this earth will pass away! The sun will burn out; the moon will be as blood; the stars will be darkened. All who remain will be the *oikos*, the house of the Lord. As the mighty crescendo of a fabulous symphony orchestra resoundingly concludes a magnificent performance, so the end comes: and "I will dwell in the house of the Lord for ever"! I will be in paradise, in fellowship with the Good Shepherd.

Monday through Friday, trying to get home at 5:00 PM is an almost impossible feat in my city. Buses and automobiles line every street for blocks. Some of the more affluent have resorted to helicopters for transportation! Watch the people closely. An air of excitement is in the air. "I've finished for the day. I'm going home!"

John Howard Payne looked out of his apartment window in Paris. For over nine years he had been away from his little hometown on Long Island. He saw the puffing buses, movement on the streets, people going home. Even though he was writing an important play, he thought of his home. He could not get it off his mind. So, he returned to his desk and wrote, "Mid pleasures and palaces though we may roam, Be it ever so humble, there's no place like home."

We see people on the streets every day. Some have no home; they have barely enough resources for lodging—one cheap bed. Others can afford to live in the most fashionable abodes in the world. The horrible tragedy is that as many face death, their only picture is one of oblivion—an unresolved question mark, regardless of their rank or station in life.

Confidence in life comes only when "the Lord is my shepherd." The end of this Psalm can be truly exclaimed by a person whose shepherd is the Lord: "I will dwell in the house of the Losd for ever." One old sheep man, writing about this phrase, said that it means, "Nothing will ever make me leave this outfit; it's great."

A little girl was asked to recite the twenty-third Psalm. The words were not accurately written on the tablets of her memory, but in her mistake there is a lesson for us all. She blurted out, "The Lord is my shepherd; that's all I want."

In South Georgia, a large family who made their living as sharecroppers usually had nothing left for luxuries or entertainment after paying the landlord and providing meager necessities. One year, the situation was different. They had planted the crops at the very best time; the rains came in generous quantity; the markets yielded the highest available prices.

The father proudly announced the good news to the family. They decided to spend some of their extra money for a gift which they could all enjoy. Carefully, they looked through the Sears-Roebuck catalog for just the right item. After a lengthy search, they chose to order a mirror.

Every day they anxiously looked for their treasure to come. Then the package arrived. Mary saw the postman leave a large parcel at the roadside mailbox. She ran and told her mother. The two of them hurried to the field to get the father and then took the long-awaited purchase inside.

The father opened it and gave the mirror to the mother for the first look. She smiled and straightened her hair as she glanced at herself in the shiny glass. Then the father inspected it—and himself— and passed the new family possession down the line of children.

Little Willie had never seen a reflection of his badly scarred face before. As a very small youngster, he had been kicked by a horse. When he saw his image, he said, "Mother, did you know I looked like this all the time?"

"Yes, Willie," his mother replied.

"And you loved me anyway?" the child inquired.

"Yes, Willie, I love you because you are mine!"

The Good Shepherd, the Lord Jesus Christ, loves us because we are his. This "Hound of heaven" wants to save every person; he wants to be our Shepherd and give us everything we need. Only when we choose him may we "dwell in the house of the Lord for ever."

Epilogue

The Lord can be your Shepherd, your Master, your Savior. He loves you and wants to give you a new life, with all the privileges of a child of the King. "For God so loved the world, that he gave his only begotten Son, that whosoever believeth in him should not perish, but have everlasting life"(John 3:16).

There is no inheritance for the person who is separated from God. "For all have sinned, and come short of the glory of God"(Rom. 3:23). "For the wages of sin is death; but the gift of God is eternal life through Jesus Christ our Lord"(Rom. 6:23).

Jesus calls us to himself: "Come unto me, all ye that labour and are heavy laden, and I will give you rest. Take my yoke upon you, and learn of me; for I am meek and lowly in heart: and ye shall find rest unto your souls. For my yoke is easy, and my burden is light"(Matt. 11:28–30).

Jesus Christ is our only way to God. Through him alone can we come into the right relationship with our Creator. "Jesus saith unto him, I am the way, the truth, and the life: no man cometh unto the Father, but by me"(John 14:6).

We must accept his word and invite him to come into our lives: "Behold I stand at the door and knock: If any man hear my voice, and open the door, I will come in to him, and will sup with him, and he with me"(Rev. 3:20). "But as many as received him, to them gave he power to become the sons of God, even to them that believe on his name"(John 1:12). You can invite Jesus Christ to come into your life right now. He will become your Lord and Savior—your Shepherd!

This prayer will help you crystallize your thoughts and have some words to use as you ask Jesus to enter your life:

O Lord, I thank you for Jesus. I ask him to forgive my sins and to come into my life. Now I thank him for coming in and commit myself into his care. I thank him for being my Shepherd! In Jesus' name, amen.

If you sincerely asked Jesus Christ to come into your life, you can be assured that he lives in you—right now!

"He that believeth on the Son of God hath the witness in himself: he that believeth not God hath made him a liar; because he believeth not the record that God gave of his Son. And this is the record, that God hath given to us eternal life, and this life is in his Son. He that hath the Son hath life; and he that hath not the Son of God hath not life. These things have I written unto you that believe on the name of the Son of God; that ye may know that ye have eternal life"(1 John 5:10–13).

Read the Bible and pray as you begin your new life. Share your decision with a church congregation in whose fellowship you will find the opportunity for growth and development in Jesus Christ.